more praise for *from spirit to matter*

Carol Lee Sanchez is a mystic who embraces the world of spirit and matter and renders them one in her poetry. Prismatic, these poems sing of the joyous and the tragic, the mundane and the eternal in life. Personal, they enlarge our thoughts about the complexities of living and loving. Prophetic, they prompt us to remember all who inhabit this world. These poems offer an oasis for the thirsty soul.

> —Carol J. Adams, author of *The Sexual Politics of Meat*

Whether we are white, black, brown, or yellow, we in America are all uprooted, cut off from the sacred power of earth ancestors' traditions. Carol Lee Sanchez helps us to envision a healing way amidst the contradictions of our lives. Blessed be!

> —Carol P. Christ, author of *Rebirth of the Goddess* and
> *Odyssey with the Goddess*

Carol Lee's poetry combines satiric wit, irony and sheer fun with profound humanistic reflection and insight. It arises from a complex context of Native and European cultures, interweaving physical and metaphysical dimensions of matter, mind, heart and spirit. Her wise words — inspired by the love of peoples and lands as well as the Trickster — carry messages of a deep-souled woman who artistically blends humor and truth with beauty and delight. She is a mezclada/mixed blood in the way she mixes the aliveness and potency of diverse cultural heritages. It is a great pleasure to enjoy this lifetime of experiences so finely crafted.

> —Mara Lynn Keller, Associate Professor,
> Women's Spirituality, Philosophy and Religion
> California Institute of Integral Studies

To read the poetry of Carol Lee Sanchez is to receive a gift of heart and mind. She is a poet whose "words are like singing", whose writing "encourages our hearts" and our minds to observe, to honor and to understand the complexity, chaos, and beauty of life. She sees the wonder in the everyday, and the irony and the humor in the extraordinary. In a world in which our imaginations are often stunted by the cruelty, desperation, fear and greed that marks much of our society, the poetry of Carol Lee Sanchez is a tonic — a ringing challenge to acknowledge and use our power in the service of life. In her writing we see a celebration of goodness that is as complex as any analysis of perversion, dysfunction and cruelty, for she writes of a vital celebration of life, one unmarred by sentimentality, pretension or self-righteousness. Read her work and laugh at yourself and life; read her work and find the courage to love, hope and heal.

> —Sharon Welch, author of *A Feminist Ethic of Risk*

carol lee sanchez
(message bringer woman)

from spirit to matter
new and selected poems
1969-1996

taurean horn press
san francisco

published by Taurean Horn Press
Library of Congress Catalog Card Number: 96-61781
ISBN 0- 931552-09-5
© 1997 by Carol Lee Sanchez
Printed in the United States of America

this book is dedicated to my children:
paul frederick, suecarol and miguél ráshid
with my love and thanks for choosing to
accompany me on this earth journey.

contents

acknowledgements ix
author's note x
prologue 1
meditation 2
symbols 3
migrations ·4

time warps

. . .prologue 6
. . .time warps 1-13 7
. . .epilogue 20
from **conversations from the nightmare**
. . .the poster invites me to take 22
. . .they have disappeared me 24
. . .up the downside of anywhere 26
. . .we have mounted 27
the last days of the monarchs (1-9) 28
country girl cityscapes (1-13) 40
from **message bringer woman**
la tienda 55
tribal chant 61
the way i was 63
vieja encantada 66
viejo 68
. . .a cry soft in dreams 69
premonition 70
echoes 72
crystals from dialogues (1-6) 73
in transition 81
yesterday 83
street fairs & hierarchies 84
yo quiero cantar 88
the exiles 91
the cry 95
through the microscope (1-11) 99
whistle stops 109
from **excerpts from a mountain climber's handbook**
from crystal 139
song of the four winds 140
this is my body 141
the two worlds of the red nations 144
coral woman's song 146
squash blossoms 148

notes from san francisco

. . .i walk blinded and a new skyscraper 151

tomorrow's history 152

dogma of anywhere (1-2) 153

dialogue: subjunctive mode 155

the song: the dance: the poem (1-3) 157

wolf stories (1-3) 160

flint stories (1-6) 162

fox tales (1-4) 167

old medicine stories (1-6) 171

journeys i, ii, iii 179

notes from central california (1-2) 195

from **she) poems** 209

she) poems ii 217

notes from central missouri (1-5) 229

messages

journey's end (santa barbara) 238

wind song 243

unpacking the years 245

song for the new age 247

regarding chaos and order 250

leapfrogging 251

. . .elemental happenstance 252

sir philip sidney reflects 254

corners and sidewalks 255

saturday's children 257

on reading of your death in poetry flash 259

on poetics 261

recitations 262

snapshots 263

celebrating women's stories 264

memo to myself 265

from spirit to matter 266

about the author 267

acknowledgements

grateful acknowledgement is made to the following anthologies in which the poems noted first appeared, sometimes in different forms:

Callaloo: journey's end (santa barbara); unpacking the years
Cosmos (england): crystals from dialogues 5
Coyote Was Here: the song: the dance: the poem
Returning the Gift: wind song; notes from central california
Y'Bird: crystals from dialogues 6

acknowledgement is also made to the following publications and since more than one or two poems were selected from each of them they are listed on the contents pages rather than on this page

Conversations from the Nightmare (Casa Editorial-1975)
Message Bringer Woman (Taurean Horn Press - 1977)
excerpts from A Mountain Climber's Handbook (Taurean Horn / Out
    West Limited - 1985)
She) Poems (Chicory Blue Press - 1995)

my heartfelt thanks to mary alice mclaughlin and thomas allen for their help in choosing poems to include in this collection that have appeared in print elsewhere and to nina freed for some very helpful feedback on a selection of poems i edited for this manuscript. and thank you josephine miles, wherever you are, for planting early seeds of confidence in my work.

author's note

in a way, all thought originates in spirit and so the thoughts that build these poems are, in my view, a gift from spirit and through me they become "hard copy" or matter — as words printed on a piece of paper. this collection not only contains selected poems published previously in small press volumes as well as anthologies, but a body of unpublished work originating in 1969 and spread through the 70's and 80's culminating with newer works from the 90's. i began writing seriously in my early 30's and this collection of poems reflect the stages of my personal and social consciousness during each decade. the "country girl cityscapes" series, for example, chronicles some memorable aspects of the transitions of a country girl from new mexico who moved to california physically, mentally, psychically and socially to live in the city by the bay. i remained there from 1964 to 1985.

time warps introduces my brand of humor and speaks to the 'new age' — "the dawning of the age of aquarius"and the spiritual seeking that surfaced on the west coast in the late 60's and early 70's. *song for a new age* recapitulates *time warps* with an additional note of wry humor pointing out the most common practices of the 90's. (i need to laugh at myself — particularly when i take myself tooooo seriously! living is "fraught" with humor as well as being <u>serious</u> business!!) *fox tales, flint stories* and *wolf stories* present another humorous phase.

my mixed race, multicultural heritage works through my poems over the years as the issues of the times rise and fall within them, but those issues are generally rooted in my background. my own discoveries about myself, my life's wonders and tragedies as well as the lives of others also lie in these poems — sometimes deeply embedded — sometimes floating on the surface as in *mezclada* or *yo quiero cantar* or *the way i was.*

these poems then are what i 'bring' into hard copy, from spirit to matter. my 'messages' from where i am here to where you are — there. i look forward to hearing from you through the pages of time.

prologue

message bringer woman
came i, into this dimension
this mattered reality
filtered through
many layered substance
to sing
these rainbow songs

meditation

i go within
into the darkness
of all that is
leave substance and
habit elsewhere

i touch
eternal consciousness
with the tips of
my imagination
want only to know
timeless sensation in
an ongoing present-

that powerful now
known to the ancients-
those spirit relatives
holding rain drops
to quench my
soul's thirst.

symbols

symbols release energy
move from mind to matter
matter very much
become stored knowledge
precious entities
collected as beads or bytes
restored on recycled trees

somewhere long ago
on an ordinary day
a human mind perceived
nature's random paintings
as recorded reflections of
familiar things

wind prints on sand or
water marks on rocks
holding line and shape
together to form: animal
fish fowl tree branch leaf
human faces human bodies

somewhere on earth
on an ordinary day
a human hand understood
the magic of transcription
used stick stone and bone
to etch symbols from her mind
into wood sand and stone

migrations

they say)   the people
went out from
            this place

they say)   the clans
left markers of
            earth bones

they say)   each clan's signature
was carefully laid
thoughtfully etched
            in stone

they say)   all those
temples, churches, cairns
encode the lives
            they lived

they say)   those markers
will tell us:
            who they were
            why they left
            where they went

they say)   those earth bones
hold the stories
hold the memories
            of all the clans

they say)   they are waiting
for us to unravel
the mysteries of
            their journeys

they say)   they are waiting
for us to follow them
            home.

time warps

prologue

forever lines the road ahead.
time fills up spaces
whatever will— will be willed—
the certainty of nothing always present.

beside a stream
or perhaps within the water
lie all the answers so long hidden.
he walks in secret solace
mourning the lost worlds
he once came from.
they are no more except
in dream memory.
no longer do strange ships
ferry passengers there
from here.
all the maps are lost
or destroyed.
he walks alone
into nowhere
into the spaces of
in-between.

1.
he rode a midnight freight out of yesterday
holding the tao in his hands
bowed sedately to the board of directors
put a nickel in the pinball machine
and tilted the universe
          with the first ball.

gentlemen, i find it difficult to
take this discussion seriously
          (he quipped
let's all meet tomorrow in the
shower at the end of the hall
and discuss the line up for
next week's game of red rover.

2.
much later
on a more prominent world
donned in the most fashionable
guise of the day—
carrying a prepared speech
in his hand
he approached the guardian manu
with as much humility as he could muster.

eyes lowered
he defiantly thrust the speech toward the manu
which promptly disintegrated —upon touch.
twisting the smile on his face
slightly to the left
immediately dissolved his disguise
leaving the manu hopelessly confused-
with no possible means of
identification.

3.
it was the gold standard
that bothered him most.
how could he possibly transfer
his acquired goods from
one universe to another
if all these idiots insisted on
quibbling over drams and grams
      and ounces.
      and the lists!
marks for this and that
and none of it
important enough to haggle over.
      but the principle was!
the principle of the thing
goaded him beyond endurance.
who did they think they were to
question the worth of **his** sharpshooter badge?
he valued it highly
it had cost him a lot
to get it!

4.
journal entry — eon 11
the visions are the worst part of universe hopping.
you can never really be sure
when they're going to turn into solid matter.
        it's all so **un**civilized.
especially the group sessions.
start combining strange currents and
you come up with short circuits!
of course it all depends on the view point.
        i can only voice mine
which is limited to my own perceptions
but **mine** under any circumstances.

i'm not adverse to a little fun now and then
but to go all out with nightmare horrors
then turn the whole damn thing into solid—
well—that's something else again.
        it was the dumps i objected to.
i'm not altruistic—and there are some
backward races around —(to play with
        when one gets bored i suppose
but that was a hell of a mess to make
        3-dimensional!
probably take another thousand or so
to clean up. sure spoiled a nice vacation spot.
        (for tripping and all that.
i just may turn in my membership card
and lone it from now on. i'll get nailed
for rebellion sure as hell—but they'll
        have to catch me first.

5.
what was it that old man sd to do?
every old man has some secret knowledge
of some kind—some cureall recipe for
        all the ills of creation.
but this one
now this one sounded a whole lot different
actually screwier than others i've heard.
he just might know what he was talking about.
didn't lay claim to being sacred either.
        that's a change!
        pyramid—
something about a pyramid.
wish i hadn't gotten so ripped last night
damn—and in alien territory too!
nobody at group will believe this story!

the mule he hung onto snorted once
before coming to a sudden stop—
        almost dislodging him.
there, in front of him, massive and solid
        stood a pyramid.
slipping to the sandy surface
he began to climb the face of it
weaving back and forth
not certain which direction to aim for.
he finally reached the capstone.
his eyes blazed with remembrance!
carefully arranging himself in proper stance
he did a slow pirouette on the point
then — leaped into **the eye**
        just as it blinked shut.

the mule collapsed in the sand
with the loudest **h e e — h a w**
he had ever **hee-hawed**
in his life.

6.
the temple
was the first thing
he saw at breakthrough.
it was massive—almost
consuming the entire land area.
the major portion of it was faced
in stainless steel along with some
clear material here and there—
      glass maybe.
the dome was a huge gyrating
plastic bubble studded with sequins!
it was almost as dazzling as the spire.
the spire was the most eyecatching part
      of the entire complex.
a solid gold penis
right in the center of the dome
emitting streams of rainbow lights
      every five seconds that
arched downward to form an umbrella of
multicolored rays over the whole temple.
as soon as the colors touched
      the ground surface
they crackled like sparklers.

as he approached the entrance
he wondered who had conceived it.
it had to be a genuine replica of
      a norman mailer dream!
who else could come up with so
      much ostentatious macho?
no matter.
here it was—and here he was
      and **he**
      intended to explore it.

7.
fade outs were always perplexing.
from solid to shadow to nothing!
it resembled molecular disintegration—
      only it wasn't.
just simple dispersion.
or so he'd been told.
but if you happened to be near
some reflective material of any kind
it was a bit disconcerting to
      watch yourself disappear.
at least **he** never got used to it.
he supposed there were some old hands
      (really old ones
in the **life adventure cycle** that
were so accustomed to it—it didn't
      bother them at all.

in-between
was more or less the best part.
no activity or need for any.
      the resting period—
      (if you could really call it that.
strange he should be thinking about **fade out**.
he'd never bothered before —
it was an accepted part of his choice.
      always there.
      like thought was.
in-between **was** a relief. gave him time to
assimilate his adventures in thought cycles.

where the hell **w a s** **in**-between??

8.
the tunnel was waiting.
a black velvet sensation filled the
expanse of its gaping mouth—
inviting him to enter.
fearful—
but still filled with expectant adventure.
he found it almost impossible to
pass one up without exploring it.
he wondered sometimes
just what he expected to find
and what it was that drove him
           into that yawing entrance—
into the warm dark interiors of caves and labyrinths.
maybe it was the secretiveness of them
and always the hope that no one else
had ever been there before—
           that he would be the first
           to be enclosed
in that warm silky blackness.
that thick moist air that stroked his senses.
           a sedative. a tranquilizer.
           he stared at the opening.
his head reeled as he perceived the mouth
reaching out to him—expanding imperceptibly.
a surge of excitement raced across his
           nervous system and
he could restrain himself no longer.

he stumbled
as he half ran to the entrance then
abruptly dissolved into the richly scented
darkness of the interior.

9.
his pupils dilated and
his breaths came in short gasps.
s h e was beautiful.
a perfect package of desirable body form
under a transparent filmy garment.
was she a vision?
or was she a dimensional figurewarp?
he had to find out quickly before
        he suffocated with want!
but how to be sure? and after he found out—
what if she spurned him?
how would he survive that?
as he slowly approached the exquisite **she**
he noticed her fully ripe lips parting to reveal
iridescent teeth perfectly shaped
and one jade tinted eyebrow
arched in almost wonder.
the pit of his stomach collapsed on itself
as he felt the hot rush of blood
        settle in his groin.
did he dare talk to her? he was just close
enough to see his reflection in the depths of
        her violet eyes.
his mouth tried desperately to form
some sort of speech when he realized
        IT was happening.
all he could do was think now.
overriding his angry frustration
he could hear her rich laughter.
        it was melodious.

just before total dispersion took place
she spoke in clear bell tones:
        cosmic reality makes sense
        if you drop the **s** from cosmic

and the fullness of her laughter
exploded all around him as
        he faded into   **in**-between.

10.
he was going to have to locate
                a **master manu**.
that's all there was to it.
he was damned tired of being whisked
here and there with very little choice
                on his part. well—
the original choice had been his
but after that—he'd had practically no
say at all!! he knew fade out could be controlled.
                t h e y could.
might cost him a bunch of credits—but
he'd had enough of this trip!
he was willing to pay whatever the cost.
this willynilly come and go
                wasn't fun anymore.
                it was tiresome.
                and frustrating.
he never got to stay anywhere long enough
                for more than just a taste.
it was beginning to make him feel hungry
all the time. he knew he should be satisfied—
                look at all the fun he'd had.
all the strange and exotic sights.
                the exciting adventures.
lord he was tired. so awfully tired.
                what was wrong with him?
had to start somewhere—and finding a **manu**
seemed to be the first step to ending this awful
feeling of no purpose. had to find out if
there's anything beyond this. there just had
to be—otherwise what was the purpose of
                the almighty **manu's**?
                and **fade outs**?
                and **in**-betweens?

11.
he cocked his head toward a being called: **saint**
and mused to himself under his breath—
      (what kind of horseshit is this?
an application form filled with insane questions!
universal bureaucracy drives me mad.
i'd raise a ruckus if i didn't need
      something from them right now.
i just don't believe this!
      who made you? name the 7 loki of
      the fifth bardo. what color is west wind?
      what is the covenant?
      how did mordacai arrive in the west?
      what did the ankh symbolize?
      give detailed information on the lotus
      and all symbology connected to it.
      who comprises the trinity?

(what has any of this got to do with applying
for a position in the service of the resident **manu**?
      how did i get myself into this?

the being called: **saint** adjusted the folds in his robe
cleared his throat to attract attention
then began to glare at him—

he looked up from the application and mumbled
in apologetic tones—
i don't seem to have any of this particular
information programmed—sir—saint—sir.

the being called: **saint** —nodded a saintly nod
smiled serenely and replied)
      well then i'll give you a pass
to the universal library and when you
have completed your studies you may return to
us for further help and guidance.

12.
it was easy to understand the saint trip.
didn't require much extended knowledge
mostly training in how to say **no**
   all the time.
the follow up could get sticky
because there was always a large group around
to yell things like:
     chicken. sucker. fanatic.
     goodiegoodie.
     holierthanthou.
and variations based on testing one's ability to
    say **no**.
good times and excessive practice of all
possible groupie practices was what a
saint tripper was conditioned to avoid.
becoming a good times groupie could cost
a solid gold halo (not just the 14 carat one
a decent—but contaminated human could earn)
a n d —a planetary directorship!!
that was a heavy loss for an apprentice saint
whose total fast from worldly life
earned him that specific reward.
sounds ridiculous—i mean—
why work your way to saint on a world
inhabited with everything you
    had to avoid—
    couldn't get involved with—or else!
the system director must have a weird sense of humor.

he continued to ponder on the conditions of the
system he was applying for so he studied the
microfilm information units.
    all this—just to fill out a
stupid application form. just to get the information
i need to control my **own** *f a d e o u t s !*
    ok— i'll do it.
just so i can find out who set this thing up.
    and when i do—

13.
he did a half gainer into the swordfish pool
bubbling his way to the other side
      —you've got to understand
      what i'm trying to talk about!
      this is a new seed i carry
      in my hand.

*   *   *time and more time*   *   *
so much time*   *   *to be born*   *   *over and over.
(but the difficulty in sprouting is obvious.

worlds away from here
two suns are e*x*p*l*o*d*i*n*g
to recombine into one light
and one heat.
they have to feed on each other
to do that.
and you walk this demon world
with no memory of tomorrow
expecting yesterday to
return once a week
with sunday brunch!

      we **have** the molecule—i tell you!
      and we're going to drop it
      on your heads whether
      you like it or not!!

*   *   *and he turned his back on them
and stepped into the pot of quicksand at
the end of the rainbow.

epilogue
on the other side of the halfway mark
down a terribly long long hall
sits a dark painted door
with letters in light
which quite simply say:

**"no one may enter through this door
who has not been here before."**
and underneath in flashing red
an arrow pointing left.
an archway enters the tunnel there
ambles on for about a mile
ending abruptly in a sharp right turn
where sits another door
painted as before!
behind that door
sits a long narrow room
turned sideways to be sure
and on the opposite wall
sit three more doors
plainly marked—but taking turns
to display their message
from left to right, as follows:

**this is the dying room
this is the lying room   and
this is the living room.**

above these doors
hang the usual signs:
exit & no smoking please
but in the very center
above all the rest
flashing yellow on the wall
the following direction relates:

**only one exit may you choose
as entrance to the beginning.**

from **conversations from the nightmare**

the poster invites me to take
a trip to the museum:

**native americans on display
pueblo - paiute - apache
in authentic native costumes!
lecture by museum guide.**

those potteries rest
in glass cases
to haunt museums.
   they concentrate
   a formal essence
a geometry of understanding
from another place.

that navajo rug on the wall
those costumes described to you—
not as clothing still worn
for a particular occasion
but- as theatrical accoutrements
for these isolated dramas—
   re-enacted.
"they'll sell anything these days"
  (she sd
she was right — not intending to be.
reminded by those gaudy signs
riding west on highway 66
when we were young:
     **next stop +++
     water + cactus candy**

**+++ see real indians make
authentic indian jewelry +++**

those gaudy signs that still lead
to every junk curio store
filled with degrading imitations of
everything dear and sacred to us:
    cardboard tom toms
    felt headbands with
    chicken feathers for
    little big chiefs

                    rubber tomahawks
genuine   plastic and tin jewelry
and i shiver looks at
the posters **we** create
as another grey line bus
pulls away from
taos la fonda to:

+++ see the indians at the pueblo +++

they have disappeared me
as they have done to all
my ancestors before me.
are you watching?

when i wear a modified
version of the traditional dress
of my pueblo tribe
it is not familiar to those
outside the southwest
but it **is** real!

look close
i may vanish
before your very eyes.

it is not a pocahontas dress.
i do not wear feathers
or a headband
or beaded moccasins
because my tribe
does not wear those things.

each tribe adapted
various forms of european
beads and ruffles and braids
that became 'traditional'
ceremonial dress by
the late seventeen hundreds
but they are indian!
because: **we** wear them!
because: **we** put them together
in a certain way.

are you watching?
i may be disappearing
right now
it keeps happening
when i remind you who i am

and pretty soon
you don't see **me** anymore—
because: i'm a left over primitive
and you're supposed to
feel sorry for me
because:
        i am poor and
        diseased and
        ignorant and
        alcoholic and
        suicidal.

you see how it happens?

what goes on in your mind
when you see any of us
wearing our ceremonial dress?

we have **not** been terminated
or exterminated.
we are here
all around you.
but—
you disappear **us**
everyday!

are you watching?

up the downside of anywhere
nobody really gives a shit.
oppressive measures of any dosage
require large quantities of
antidotes: larger than attitude shifts
exclusively adjusted to this point
or that.
solitary confinement eludes the best
of us but belongs always
to the edge of everything.
you are not expected to comprehend
the trends of any patterns until
they are inconclusive statistics
at which point — they will be
charted, graphed and affixed to
all memory banks immediately.
plundered minds respond to looting
with amiable reflex in these times
deciding that all purposeful intent
can be set aside during reclamation
proceedings.
disguised soothsayers maintain order
in spite of all traumatic situations
lying scattered about in the streets.
intruders come and go at will
pick up bits of glass
cast their reflections into them
at random
then throw them at
the local passersby for
future collections.

we have mounted
the burning ash
and counted jawbones
in the pits of

darkened dead
and dying all around.

our stripéd bombs
a-bursting comfort
and ease
trip through
the red white and blue of

darkened dead
and dying all around.

melted leaves will
mix with bones
carrion fish will
travel far
to cover this dust
and ash of

darkened dead
and dying all around.

a concrete
high-rise tombstone
old glory and napalm
phnom-penh and

darkened dead
and dying all around.

the last days of the monarchs

1.
the problem is vague—
personify the point of view
that existence   doesn't
and extend the perspective of
eleventh century retablos in a direct line—

connect it with hard/edge
        pop/op —   **2-d**
and consider that half of 4 is 2
then   the second dimensional flatness
is relative
related to everything that doesn't exist.

the point of reference dissolves into
the problem beside the shadows
that disappear—
the absence of light precludes the lack
of linear direction.
shapes contain volume—
cannot be contained inside
or outside of any descriptions:
their solidity remains as outlines
melted into planar perception—
no light to describe the edges.

the thick or thin of anything
cannot be described to the mind
with signs from the hands.

2.
disband the archetypes to
warp the muses into
mechanics disgorging
siren songs of the centuries
paraded in cement.

replay tyrants in royal purple
with crimson headed doctrines
pasted to their teeth.

fight for your life—
it's all you have left
to call your own
beyond electronic output
and memoried input.

what was implicit then
will become explicit
when somebody notices
the pattern of usual
ordinary events.

3.
upstairs, on sanitation level—
department squads left the
program area to apply for
understatement of the year.

the magnum-at-large walked
along corridors designed for
maximum security but was
detained by incompetent thrifters
demanding higher thrift shops
and lower department stores.

the shock absorbers along the
main thoroughfares continued to
take up the meaningful slack—
keeping track of maladjustment
syndrome and improper balance.

learnéd institutions predicted the
daily rates of being, consumption
and waste; produced new graphs of
intimidation to equalize
demand and barter.

the 'for instance box' computed
daily quotas of specific weathers
and humors to be radiated into
the tracking system and maintenance
teams drilled holes every hour
to count the treasury's decline.

4.
correlate pliny in the numerical
succession of masters to any throne
available at any progressive point
in history and you will understand
the movement of monarchs (he sd

to introduce any system to the
violation of the arbitrary laws
that define its limitations is to
demonstrate the function of obsolescence.
no arbitrary system, once set up and
working in an organizational capacity
can conceive of itself as ever be
coming obsolete   —or defunct.

obsolescence is entropic due to:
inefficiency, lack of innovation
and the hard fast dogmatic rules
that lead to crystallization, rigidity
and consequent demise   (he concluded.

5

to preserve the triumphs of any
civilization, the mad hatters and
the fakers must be sifted out,
mummified and displayed as they were.
what is left is then distilled and
we find a few grains of precipitated
salt crystals.

"Despite the turmoil the process continued
although the implications were such, that
more involvement was actual than primarily
indicated. presumably, any social order that
directs itself to the preservations of freedoms
for the individual —inevitably begins systematic
legislation to protect personal interests, then
large groups to control small groups. These grow
into monopolies to lobby legislators sworn to
protect the rights of individuals. this has be
come a corporate social structure composed of
nameless faceless once individuals who still
believe in their individual rights as separate
identities to man the corporate robot. on the
other side the legislators group themselves into
a bureaucratic robot and the two square off and
declare war on each other based on this
freedom of choice concept and individual
rights—"   (he sd

the salts, magnified, examined in minute
microscopic detail —indicated this
traumatic pattern. one such civilization
dubbed this peculiar pattern:

free enterprise

6.

"enhance the major determinations with
popularity polls in order to demonstrate the
intrinsic worth of being in any given society.
question the ability to arrive at any qualified
opinion pertaining to the descriptive enclosure
of a particular mind set. within those bounds,
eliminate then, all prior judgements, preconceived
notions and justifiable biases that cannot
possibly be fitted to those specific confines.
to legislate human integrity on a pound per
pound basis is to annihilate human
value altogether"   (he sd

"the unqualified mechanisms that operate
any system are never questioned until the
robotic end results display the long term
overactive concern of legislative bodies
determined to water down, but not entirely
wash out —all necessary human contradictions.
civilized methodologies tended to suppress and
repress in varying degrees rather than to
upraise or reaffirm consciousness within the
majority populace of all civilizations now
terminated"   (he concluded.

**the juxtaposition of this information is
designed to instruct. the prime factors
equalize and distribute civilized justice
in some orderly fashion based on the
arbitrary laws imposed by each system
so demonstrated. . . . . .**

7.
**it is the concern of all willing participants
here gathered— to locate the precise point
the various destruct mechanisms began to
operate —therefore describing these over
all patterns and their relationships to pin
point the irreversible momentum that lead
to the eventual demise of those civilizations
herein discussed.**

"verify then, the premise that monarchs
maintained a particular continuity, guiding
the general populace with paternal bene
volence"   (he sd

"pose the reality that monarchy reestablished
itself within the precepts of a republic, re
versing the roles of monarch and subjects.
the format of charter and constitution merely
redefined inalienable human rights, although
the equitable protection of these, were em
bodied in an abstract concept termed: **law**.
the powers of the ancient monarchs and the
later figureheads called: **presidents,
premiers,** or **primeministers**—   remained
basically the same— though surface appearances
of humanness rather than divinity maintained
by the monarchs, disarmed the populace into
acceptance of these subtle redefinitions.
the paternal benevolence continued to be
meted out on the basic tenets of:
**the good of the people, the welfare of
the masses, the welfare of the state.**
all biases and human differences were mostly
ignored —or observed with resignation —or
received with strained silence and termed
out of order.
many systems attempted to modify and
produce a uniformly conditioned mindset
to ensure the perpetuation of monarchs.
the right of passage to the throne also
underwent many alterations in order
to confuse the masses.

from title through blooded lineage
to selection from the ranks of the
commoners   —the final
result was always an only slightly
modified variable of the only
precedent example of government
on that planet:

that of the **monarchs"**   (he concluded.

8.

    this particular structure
carried with it
the momentum of collapse
carefully built in:
bricked
mortared
pasted
plastered
notarized in gold seals.
graven images
conquered in bronze,
to remind them
they must reward heroes—
burn memorial incense
collected out of battlefields:
blood caked to
smoke in remembrance.

"queued and silent, staring faces
wait for the nothing. the final
moment that came with no sound
caught in these holograms—
all that was left to us
as record of the collapse."

    the answer never
emptied out of the
communication networks. ·
no movement.
they crystallized in place.
no mass hysteria.
no human agony.
no vibrations came
to alter the
historic hologram.

"these historic documents will be
on display in the archives for
further scrutiny. chemical
analyses can be taken for
determination of food staples
ingested beyond the obvious

diets of corpses as shown.
legumes show up to some
extent and a common plant
called: strawberries.
some olfactory tests can be
made but limited equipment
will not give refined separations.
the odor of collective terror
will overwhelm you at first
but continue the separations—
there will be some subtle
odors to classify"   (he sd

9.
this enervated cabbage leaf
proclaims the dilemma
we all face

         just stands there
         and sums it all up.

confound the noun!
and   the sealing wax—
energetic adjectives   be damned!
         i'll tell the story
         of slips and slides
and the playmates of the kings.

those castle keeps are cold and damp
like musty steins of stale beer
         and **oh**
         beware the giant
         tarantula
         inside the dungeon hold—
not like those miniature oysters shelled
to serve the man who weeps.

this manger
cannot hold the hay of hell or
half the staw behind the door—
         but chaff
         it finds in mounds
         and heaps
to feed the worthy
verbed and ready
who would argue with this tale!

country girl cityscapes

1.
cherry blossoms turn green
to match the hillside.
grotesque palm trees stretch
in front of me
layered with smoked greys
while beneath me
the ribbon i follow is only
shades darker.
i travel through another
time warp and disappear into
the here and now of a fruit juice
special harvey wallbanger
         -wall banged her into the wall
lamp bulbs dribble across purple carpet
         explode against beer cans
with a paper sack pop well aimed.
the falling fragments mirror an
ego encrusted old man
asking me to like him
         —hello there, you knock me out-
just to like his ice cold snow white hair
         and frozen sensibilities.
he spreads a deep freeze around us
and we become half thawed tuna for
next friday's dinner because we still
cannot shout down age determined
         to go on forever.

2.
a circus lights up inside my head
carousel music spins me into a
barker with long-handled mustache
and top hat:
         step right up folks!
         step into my arena here-
I'll demonstrate marvelous feats of
daring— adventure —thrills & chills
         up & down your spine—

my spine tingles when you
look at me intensely but
i cannot see what you are saying.
i see only the colors that
fall from your mouth.
      syncopated rhythms spiral
out of your throat— funnel into your
finger tips dancing along my thighs
until i almost forget the neon sign
      flashing blue
      flashing red
      flashing green
outside my bedroom window.
somewhere out of present time
      you say you should have
been a drummer or learned to
play a musical instrument.

my body is a mellow instrument
finely tuned— waiting only for
      the concert to begin.
you are a fine musician.
universal rhythms flow through
your soul into your hands and into
      your loins.
you cradle me in your arms and
begin your song of life.
      your music rushes
through me and i can sing your love
with my body
      sing your happiness
      your successes-
then i can cry your sorrow - your failure
echo your fear -seethe with your hate.
the concerto flows on and on
      into a rondo
      a scherzo
weaving the melody, building the theme
      higher -faster -faster
      andante -**andante**
      finale.

3.
fantasies collide with memory
impossible to unravel the mess.
easier to lie here and think it
        all at once—over indiana.
chicago to our left- pittsburgh
        to our right
new york- dead ahead.
i rocket through time and space
into layers of cloud fluffs
casting shadows below.
i **am** my solar plexus mixed with
        your voice—deep and soft
calling me to you in that future point.
i roll time forward in my thoughts
backward in my memory
converge into that particular time
we discovered each other.
i loved you unselfishly (i sd
expected only your soul in return.
that wasn't too much to ask
since you don't believe in immortality.
we still cast shadows with our thoughts
into our separate realities.
the theory of conservation is relative
to all of this—someplace   in some
        dimension or plane.
i am sleepy. but i won't let go yet.
there is something i wanted to
        remember about earlier.
i am confused trying to determine
which earlier i wanted to recover-
to find something i discovered back
there—that seemed important to
know about. another kind of awareness
crashes through the whirling scenarios of
yesterdays half-lived / full speed / **whoa!**
can't see you in my mind!
the mirror is cracked!!

4.
shards of colored light
come into focus behind my eyelids
extend themselves

     whirl forward
from the black depth of nowhere
tear across my nervous system
rush through my blood stream
     grow larger
in shape and form
     finally reach my brain
     only to **explode**.

i fall asleep as a steady rain of
glass falls behind my eyes.
     i will look for
the floor it fell on in the morning.
i am reluctant to receive the
bombardment of old memories
uniting with the moment i re-
     experience you.

5.
experience. become aware! get in touch.
get in touch—touch—touch. i wanted to
touch the lump of flesh between your
thighs—i wanted to feel the slow
steady growth of a solid form in my hand

you moved away—
remembered all the castration myths invented
by the sterile philosophers of our time
and times long gone. greedy men—
holding onto their seed—to their feces—
-saving it up like dollars
     in a vault intent on frustrating
     nature's living cycles.

hiding from knowledge that they too
will finally burst underground

43

like over-ripe melons and rot
        back into the cycle-
        and still they have
disciples and followers who use precious
brain cells to compute every possible
way to disguise the reality that
        i woman **am** receptacle
        and nourisher of sentient
human life on our planet.
i am sad to know you believe those myths
you might understand if you accepted
what they refuse to acknowledge—but
it makes little difference
        their copper-lined oak covered
        coffins will decay just the same
and you and i will continue our lovemaking—
pretend we didn't notice that little
slip back into mythology. i will reach
        to touch you again
        you will attempt to respond
with a new mode of self-awareness invented
        by the beatles
        spiced with a dose of dylan
        and baez
        twentieth century mythologists
creating contemporary myths to hand down
to a new era.
i wonder who will replace margaret mead?

6.
and the new legends might read something like—
        in the beginning
        there was **sound**
a single pure **sound** that filled up the void.
after many ages the **sound** spread out from
itself and formed separate vibrations   and
        the vibrations were **sound** and
        the **sound** was **vibration**
and the **vibrations** chased after one another
in all of space—around and around for many

more ages then
> these **vibrations** gathered
> themselves up into the **sound**
> and the sound reexperienced
> itself and in a pure ecstacy
> broke apart and reformed
> into **eight single tones**.

the tones discovered themselves and their
ability to make separate sounds
at different intervals.
they were so delighted
they sounded themselves
> again and again
> bounced against each other
> through time and space
> creating a wondrous melody
> and **the cosmos** began. . .

7.
music. numbers. geometry. circles.
> squares. triangles—boxes
> —tubes of time.
you sd) we shouldn't get involved with
each other too seriously because we didn't
know one another yet. we should wait
> a year —or two —or three—
and see if we still feel the same.
but in the meantime you would like to
live with me and share my bed and be free
to have other friends.
> and i sd)—
> what did i say?
that was long ago as i measure time.
i remember that you did live with me
> for awhile— and had your
other friends too —women friends
because you had to talk to other women
to make you feel good because your head
was so fucked up—but i was the best

45

the only one who understood you
understood—**you**-
and you— **and you**—

click-**click**. a metal tube snaps into place
around me —floats me onto the pink-and-green
merry-go-round-pony.
i can almost reach the brass ring.
next time around i will. but first i have to take the
carey bus to manhattan and the barry bus to
san francisco to spend a lot of time in
bus terminals train stations and airports.
someday—i'll spend an equal amount of time
on ship piers saying hellos and waving goodbyes.
    kiss me—because i like the way
    you kiss.
    it's very sensual.

take a risk. make an investment. invest yourself
    in **present** time!

8.
time. i am stuck in time. present time.
the here and then overlap events and people
reappear. repeat. repeat in day to day sequence.
i begin to experience horror that this is actually
    my reality. my present time—
    and not my fantasies!

how do i make it stop? how do i break the pattern?
it hurts to love one person very much. easier to
love everybody a little bit. don't explain anything.
i don't fill your expectations of sleeping beauty
and cinderella all rolled up in a neat package.
i know you can't love me—romantically—
    like in fairy tales and hollywood movies.
you are too young—and i am old—older—an
    older woman. i forgot how old
i seem to younger people once i passed the
    quarter century mark.

i will not accept your judgements or your words!
it's a oneway street and i'm alone on it.

later? maybe. did you say later?
i may not be in this place— later.
futures are for stockbrokers and fortunetellers.
i'm done with probing futures.
that cantankerous old man named fritz sd:
swing with your pain. told me to get right down
inside and really experience **pain!**
i don't want to
how can i ?
i learned to avoid and avoid. avoid and vanish,
that's what happened!
I vanished before my eyes and i couldn't find out
where i'd gone.
another young man sat in front of me and
asked me where i was going and
i sd) right here.
but i forgot to tell him   —i'd already left.

9.
sand blows across the desert in a series of funnels.
mud houses disappear into a haze of finely
shaded ochres and umbers.
the landscape is continuous.
it stretches on and on—familiar—comfortable
defiantly untamed.
i want to go there again and walk barefoot
across the dry—almost naked soil.
i want to climb a massive sandstone cliff
sit silently on top—let wind whip through
my clothes to cool my body.
just sit there and let sand scour my face.
fill my nostrils and eyelashes.
i want to
hug my solitude as my eyes take in every detail.
tears of memory sting my eyes
but i won't let them fall

it makes me angry when i cry for stupid reasons
       and stupid losses.
sometimes—i miss my native land—i miss it
even more when i come across a door marked:
       lonely—in my mind.

we lie next to each other — our bodies heated
and shiny. i am bobbing in a sea. the rhythms
of waves lull me into a deep unknowing until
the fine thread of your voice reaches down
encircles me—and pulls me up from the deep
into the real. what is it —i mumble through
hazy—glow. **snap**. to—to what? real pain?
       i wanted to know then.
something is missing (you sd.
something that would make it complete.
it makes me angry to cry. remembering.
and angrier —when i remember words
instead of the joy and excitement we shared.
and this moment?
what of this moment in time?

10.
a heaviness begins to settle on my chest.
my head. my shoulders.
it must be time to move again.
       i don't want to leave my bed—
but the country would be nice. windy trees and
bare ground. cricket chatter late nights.
early morning birds arguing back and forth.
far away dogs barking imagined intruders
out of deep shadows. no super highways
forcing the swish/swish/squeal of tires and brakes
       inside my tired head.
       the country would be nice.
i'm almost rooted in concrete. raw soil
alien to my barefeet. i've grown accustomed to
cement strewn with bits of shattered glass.
my feet are tough and calloused.
       i feel safe walking through

narrow canyons of steel and concrete—
marble the only godmade stone in these city
canyons.
manmade conglomerates are not very threatening.

city daylight is filtered through layers of
carbon particles and fog banks. nights are
multicolored neons, zeons and mercury lamps.
there is never complete darkness—anywhere in this
zone.
bathroom nightlight guides always remain
       in side streets and back alleys.
points of reference to use as accurately as stars
used by any mariner to plot a nighttime course.
       few stars are visible in this zone.
       it's never dark enough to see them.

i like living on this island—with bridges leading
off it into unknown places outside these canyons.
       the country is beyond the bridges.
       outside my vision.
       the bridges are always there.
i can cross over one and be in the country
       but then i will lose the bridges.
tree covered hills will hide them from me and i
won't know the boundaries of the place i'm in.

cities are peopled with loneliness—
       and we're all in it together.
       it's safe and warm.
all the people walking down all the streets
       are as lonely as i am.
       and we all know it.
and it's safe to be lonely. in the city. together.

       I walk down a street
look into an open storm drain and fall down a well
       from a childhood memory.
slimy green water rushes up at me. sucks me
under.
       warm and comforting.
i don't want to leave this place—but a sidewalk
stretches out from the bottom of the well and i

keep walking until i find my all american
      red white and blue
      pick-up truck.
i have to drive a long time to get back to my bed.

11.
drip. dry. on my freeway! flash/**yellow**.
it tastes sooooo good you can drink it straight.
yellow/flash—flash. **hammmmmmm's**—
blue/flash—**red**/flash—**yellow**/flash—**flash**.
where is the craft? it's all gone!!
      i am illiterate. i cannot read greek.
i can barely understand the sixsided bombardment of
media on my sixsided senses. six sides makes a hexagon
and hexagons make benzene rings but benzene rings
don't have diamonds in their valences.

      i had a diamond ring once.
just another gimmick—like loaded dice—to win a game
no one's sure how to play in the first place.
      the **laws** of a game
      make the **essence** of the game.
a violation of these laws would destroy the game!
      a workable premise.
i will first determine the **laws** in order to determine
      the essence. there's the catch.
what are the laws of the games i play?
the essence of my life?   the times i live in?

i live in the twentieth century in the country that
outstripped latrec outrageously! where hamburger
      coca/cola/hot/ dog signs
      flash **on** and **off**
lure me into devouring the nostalgic cardboard taste of
leftover pulp stuffed into grinders and skins
to remind me i live in america. the land of milk and
honey and polluted '**sky blue waters**' that serve up
my favorite countless brand name beers.
mountain waters fermented with atomic wastes to
give **YOU** 'the **hottest brand** going'

going—going—**gone**!
sold to the gentleman in the corner with the tall hat.
　　　　sam's the name.
and still i am illiterate—in france—in rome—in
sumeria and egypt. i cannot read sanskrit or latin!
I have american
blood in my veins. **and**—i'm a woman!

12.
grey forces its way into my awareness now.
　　　　asphalt grey. cement grey.
the color of the city canyons i live in.
i wander into the canyons and meet a
　　　　false prophet in a cave
　　　　in one of the box canyons.
he says i must be his concubine. i say **no**.
i do not believe in false prophets. he insists
i must do his bidding —because it is important.
very important and pertinent to everything.
　　　　i ask him why.
he says it will change his false prophecy into
truth and then he can take this **truth** and
　　　　give it to the people.
i ask him how he can do this—and he says i must
do these special exercises and breathe salt water
　　　　up my nose to purify my head.
he will then rub special oils made from the squeezings
　　　　of the seven grains all over my body
　　　　and then fuck me.
that will initiate me into the people's religion.
　　　　i refuse—because i am chicken.
　　　　i do not want to belong to the people.
i throw him out—but before he leaves
　　　　he gives me a secret document
　　　　in some sort of glyph which
　　　　i roughly translate as follows—

instructions for young revolutionaries:
　　　　ruminate on platitudes.

endeavor to separate the spittal
of thought from dialogue.
the victuals once devoured become
impossible to locate in the dark
tunnels of the lower digestive tract.
            alternate and fornicate.
withhold only the bones of communication
            from all heathen outsiders
            —detractors —and vacuums.
advance: into the ranks and files of
            the bureaus-at-large.
dump all drawers into the bypass.
tar and concrete all the remnant tenets.

mobilize all units.

activate all yardage and tonnage.
            compute the end result.
sit your ass down—on the curb.
s c r e w your head on **t i g h t**
            and w a i t!!
something will happen.
            —eventually!

13.
i move through the canyons again.
the motion propels me toward somewhere else.
another place to watch and wait.
a great white hunter appears in a dimly lit canyon
            stalking the night
in and out of caves—searching for the tawny-haired
            lioness who forever eludes him.
            he stalks with stiff-legged gait.
involved in a self image he does not claim as his own
he emanates his hunting abilities with elegance.
(an alien would disguise himself with more discretion.

my eyes follow all the movements
of all the separate games—hidden behind

male and female subtleties
waiting for fragments to combine. overlap.
interlock.
anything to make the patterns more interesting.

boredom is an element of dispersion.   no locus.
        no point to concentrate the energy
        scattered out from the multitudes
boredom is the center of void.
apathy has direction—if only by the sheer force of
        its downward movement.

to probe the obvious is the object of the game.
discover only that—which can be seen.
        see what you look at.
        see what you hear.
pay attention—**pay attention!**
        don't give your eyes away.
blindness is costlier than you imagine.

        and still—
        i can forbid you
        to hear me.

from **message bringer woman**

la tienda*

hand chiseled sandstone
terraced false front
born 1867
tribute to the craft
of an unremembered mason
                    'there used to be an
                    old pot bellied stove. . .'

i never saw it
but the large economy sized
coleman oil heater that
replaced it wasn't very new
and it had to be filled
twice a day to keep it going.

1.
8 o'clock opening time
the store crew stands
around the stove just long
enough to ease early
morning chill.
the old men of cubero
find their places around
it from midmorning on.

in twos or threes they
shuffle in. . .stopping at the
counter to make a token
purchase before the
daily 'junta' begins.
backsides up against the stove
gloved hands protect them
from the intense heat.
old man durand was always
first to arrive and last to leave.
his hearing aid didn't help
his hearing much, nor did the
cupped hand . . .and if he
wasn't asking someone to
repeat something he missed
he was asking them to talk louder.

the other men would finally
ignore him. . .shaking their
heads with pained impatience.

> 'he doesn't ever pay attention. . .'
> 'wants to know every word. . .'
> 'déjalo. . .leave him be. . .'

> 'rafael is in the paratroopers now. . .'
> 'augustine's brother is making
> good money in san diego. defense
> plant. too old to fight.. . .'
> 'the postmaster's boy was in that
> division on bataan. . .no word. . .
> no one knows. . .'
> 'so was begote's hijo julián. . .'
> 'qué lástima. . .'
> 'manuelito is politicking again. . .'
> 'sí. .county convention coming
> pretty soon. . .'
> and another gringo running
> for county commissioner. . .'
> 'por diós. . .we have to listen
> to those awful speeches unless
> we insist on an interpreter. . .'
> 'no lloras hombre. . .we eat more
> meat during campaigns. . .'
> 'si. . .bailes y juntas. . .the músicos
> will get paid. . .'
> 'ah sí. . .poco mas carne, pero
> siempre frijoles. . .'

lunch hour conversations done
clemente stops to get a new
sack of dúkes on the way out.
they trudge back up the road
past lauro's cantina to arrive
one by one in their adobe homes
in time for mid-day comida.

2.
afternoon sun bounces off
tall panes. . .shimmers
all around a lone gas pump
outside
warming a slab of mirror
finished concrete that
always had to be salted
in the winter.
two indian ladies sit up against
the green board store front
wrapped in their shawls
waiting for a ride down the
road to one of the pueblo
villages off the main highway.

three or four younger townsmen
hired for the day, sit, feet
dangling from the warehouse
platform. . .hand rolled smokes
hanging lazy on their lips
waiting for a carload of
flour to arrive.

an old battered pickup truck
pulls up to the pump
driven by an older white haired
acoma indian man.

                         'how's your cattle my friend?
                         ready for delivery.?'
                         'not so good my friend
                         some got pink eye. '
                         'that's not so good. . .you
                         doctor them?'
                         'i been doin all that but no help
                         these days. only old men like
                         us left to do all the work.'
                         'you bring your gas coupons?'
                         'i got them but not so many
                         left for this month. good
                         thing we still got horses. . .'

3.
june. sheepcamp time.
red chili stew and salt
pork beans bubbling in
cast iron kettles on the fire.
thick black coffee steaming
on a blue speckled enamel pot.
tin plates and cups clatter as
dark brown sheepherders lunch
in the shade of scrub cedar trees.
five sacks filled with the morning's
shearing. six, maybe seven to go.
(good yield this year. back to
the corrals to bleating sheep that
wait to lose their winter coats.
up on a platform, a man climbs
into a burlap sack suspended
between two cedar poles to
pack loose wool into place.
(should weigh out 350 pounds
if it doesn't shrink too much.
late afternoon and a dust cloud
announces the arrival of 'the store
truck' to collect the fat bags
of wool. tired men amble to
the fire, fill their coffee cups,
roll smokes and wait—
hunched on their heels'

the truck rolls to a stop
beside the wool stack.
two cubero men climb down
and begin to swing 300 pound
bags onto the truck bed.
a couple of indian men
climb on the back to help.

> 'bueno amigo. . .the patrón says
> to tell you we weigh it mañana. . .
> about 10 o'clock.'
> 'stá bién amigo. . .we be there—
> 10 o'clock.'

a years' work measured in
several thousand pounds of
wool rolls slowly back down
a rutted dirt road to be
stored in a barn til there's
a carload full.
next—it will be shipped by
rail to woolen mills on
the east coast.
a years' worth of food
and clothing for one family-
on account
at the 'old cubero store'.

4.

        'ga wa tsi'
        'tow wah eh'
        'is that you? my goodness. . .
        you're such a big girl now. . .
        how's your mama? we
        haven't seen her in a long time. . .'

deep red. . .flowered shawl. silk fringed
the special one. . .for outings. hugged close
in winter and draped behind the shoulders
in summer. . .always hiding rich black hair.

        'we used to keep you with us. . .
        do you remember?' you were so
        small, and always running away
        from your mama.'

and there was always some cellophane
wrapped rock candy in the pocket of your
checked gingham apron. the checks were
cross stitched in bright colored threads
and the smell of fresh baked bread and
wood smoke clung to the edges of it.

        'how much. . .huh tsu nats ah?
        don't you understand laguna?'
        no aunt marie.. .only a few words.'
        'shame on you.. . .you should get

59

your grandma to teach you. . .'
'i will aunt marie. . .it's good to
see you. . .'
'shrow oh.' . .well tdru ee shots. . .
we must go now. tell your
folks hello for us. and you come
to paguate sometimes and visit us.'

[*la tienda: the store;
'junta': meeting;
déjalo: leave him be;
hijo: son;
qué lástima: what a shame;
sí: yes;
por diós: dear god;
no lloras hombre: don't (cry) complain man;
bailes y juntas: dances and meetings;
músicos: musicians;
poco más carne pero siempre frijoles:a little more meat but always beans;
dúkes: dukes(tobacco);
cantina: saloon;
adobe: mud brick;
comida: meal;
bueno.. amigo: okay.. friend;
patrón: boss;
stá(from está) bien ..amigo: that's good.. friend;
ga wa tsi: hello/greetings how are you;
tow wah eh: just fine thank you;
huh tsu naht sah: how much does it cost;
shrow oh: let's go;
tdru ee shots: goodbye.]

tribal chant

yo soy índia*
pero no soy

nació mi abuela
on the reservation, a
laguna indian -but her daddy
was a scotsman
un gringo, también un anglo y
yo soy anglo
pero no soy

yo soy árabe
pero no soy

nació mi papá
en un land grant town
se llama seboyeta
en un cañyón de los
cebolleta mountains on
the east slope of mt taylor
en nuevo méjico
su papá
nació en lebanon
across an ocean
in another continent
embraced by those
gentes coloniales de méjico
spoke spanish, arabic and
finally english
pero sin facilidád.
mi papá is a seboyetano
heir to the grant
raised with mexican
spanish customs y
yo soy chicana
pero no soy.

este llanto
plays in my head
weaves in and out

through the fabric
of my days

yo soy índia
pero no soy
yo soy anglo
pero no soy
yo soy árabe
pero no soy
yo soy chicana
pero no soy

yo soy todos
de estos
culturas -y más.

[*yo soy índia: i am indian;
pero no soy: but i am not;
nació mi abuela: my grandmother was born;
un gringo: a gringo, a foreigner
también: also;
se llama: named
en un cañyón de los cebolleta: in a canyon of the onion (mts);
su papá nació en: his papa was born in;
gentes coloniales de méjico: colonial peoples of mexico;
pero sin facilidad: but without ease or facility;
este llanto: this lament]

the way i was

summer nights
august hot
rio grande valley
alfalfa blooms thick in the air-
belén fiestas* & post war
good times - the dances
at tabot's hall after
bumping & sweating in
the carpa in the plaza
-un nikle a dance-
tres dias the corrido of the day
-y linda mujer la canción
everybody sang at the
drop of another nickel
in the jukebox right
next to hank's lovesick blues
& buddy gallegos was golden
gloves that year & steve
gutierrez was going
to college -pre-med
& ted montoya was
going to georgetown
& our dreams were large
& ducktails high fashion with
pompadours and 'chukes'
y mi prima wanted to
change her name from
baca to baker because
she was a guera & neither
side would let her in &
parking along the rio on
those sticky nights in ronnie's
convertible 'making-out'
& me or my prima dolly
(who was really dorotea
would break everyone up
with our favorite chiste
right in the middle of
a french kiss:
'jou dohn kees me

cuz jou lahve me-
jou kees me cuz jou
wanna doo me sahmtheeng.'

later at the sweet shop
drinking gallons of cherry cokes
& smoking luckies riding up
& down main street in belén
hollering out of the car
windows at the guys:
'how come jou kees me
by the reever last night
& on the strit jou don't
tohld me hahllo?
-those fiestas-
puras fiestas
hermanos, hermanas felices
talk bad -talk mad
mira como eres y
jou betchu que sí

mama yo quiero
mama yo quiero
ma -maaa -yo
quiero a a-pren-de-er

later in september
fiestas in santa fe
pit roasting a cabra
in the ground y
tengo que buscar
una linda mujer.
we were all
lindas mujeres
& all the guys were
johnny chiarasquiados
& i miss those
easy days of:
echa otro nikle en
en el ni-ca-lo-di-en. . .
& affection y costumbre
mira como andas mujer
por tú querer-

growing up in
qualquier pueblo
in new mexico o tejas
or colorado o arizona
y otras partes. . .
y tengo sentimientos
for those long gone
days -easy   -lazy
days y la canción-
'. . .tengo que buscar
una linda mujer. . .'

[*fiestas: feasts;
carpa: tent;
un nikle: a nickel;
tres dias: three days; corrido: romance;
la canción: the song;
chukes: pachucos;
y mi prima: and my cousin;
guera: blond; dorotea: dorothy;
chiste: joke;
puras fiestas: pure parties;
hermanos: brothers,
hermanas felices: happy sisters;
mira como eres y: look how you are and;
jou betchu que sí: you bet that's so;
mama yo quiero: i want my mama;
yo quiero a aprender: i want to learn;
cabra: goat;
tengo que buscar: i have to look for;
una linda mujer: a pretty woman;
chiarasquiados: playboys;
echa otro nikles en: put another nickel in;
en el nicalodian: in the nickelodian;
costumbre: custom;
mira como andas mujer: look how you walk woman;
por tú querer: for your love;
qualquier pueblo: whichever town;
y otras partes: and other parts;
tengo sentimientos-i have nostalgia for.]

vieja encantada*

bewitched old woman
why do you laugh demented?
did they paint the evil eye
on your door,
whispering and pointing,
those viejitas of the town?
why do you stop
in the middle of the road
to chase those dogs away?

> 'perfetita encantada,
> vieja loca, vieja loca'
> cantaron los niños
> del campo.

> 'corre, corre,
> aqui vienen los perros
> perfetita encantada
> vieja loca del cubero.'

they bark and growl so loud
you cover your ears.
they bite and snap at your ankles,
drive tears to your eyes-
rip screams from your throat.

> 'vieja loca, vieja loca
> no hay perros en el camino-
> estate quieta vieja loca!
> andas a la tienda para
> comprar dulces
> por tú bebito.
> no lloras otra vez!'

perfetita encantada
wild-eyed vieja
with shocked white hair
running down the road, laughing
running down the road, screaming

66

running from the pack of dogs
that are not there.

'perfetita encantada, vieja loca
ha ha ha
no hay perros en el camino'

sing the children
of the town.

[*vieja encantada: bewitched old woman;
viejitas: crazy ladies;
perfetita encantada: bewitched perfetita;
vieja loca: crazy old woman;
cantaron los niños del campo: cry the children of the countryside;
corre: run;
aquí vienen los perros: here come the dogs;
vieja loca del cubero: crazy lady of cubero;
no hay perros en el camino: there are no dogs in the road;
estate quieta: be quiet;
andas a la tienda: walk to the store;
para comprar dulces: to buy sweets;
por tú bebito: for your baby;
no lloras otra vez!: don't cry anymore!]

viejo*

faded baggy pants, flannel shirt,
vino breath. 82 when we last met.
blue-eyed tears edged over red-rimmed
eyelids, a warm handshake.
                    -hace mucho tiempo. . .
through a tobacco stained toothless smile.
                    -y tús hijos? how many have you now?

white haired tokay wino. proud rock mason
broad shouldered and tall beneath that ancient cone
shaped stetson. how well you look, don braulio. . .
                    -sí, por un viejo. four generations of your
                    family i have worked for. tú abuelo elías,
                    tú abuelo narciso, tú papa, y ahora para tí.
                    yo hize las casas de su família. . .and now
                    these old eyes see your babies grow. y si
                    puedo, i will also build their houses.
                    soy viejo hijo, -pero duro!.

casas duras. adobe. cut stone. vigas.
          casas del país.
in cubero, they sd you died last winter-
alone in your casita. they sd:
                    -pues he was all alone you know. y sus hijos
                    se fueron pa' califórnia. son ricos. . .
                    en califórnia.

viejo. solo. muerto. solo.

[*viejo: old man; hace mucho tiempo: it's been a long time;
y tús hijos?: and your children?; sí, por un viejo: yes, for an old man;
tú abuelo: your grandfather; y ahora para tí: and now for you;
yo hize las casas de su família: i have builtthe houses of your family;
y si puedo: and if i can; soy viejo, hija: i am old, child;
pero duro: but strong; casas duras: strong houses; adobe: brick mud;
vigas: beams; casas del país: houses of the region; casita: little house;
pues: well; y sus hijos se fueron pa' califórnia: and his children went to
california; son ricos: they are rich.; solo: alone; muerte: he died.]

a cry, soft in dreams, murmurs
        of a shallow laugh
        once cold and white.
shadows move into memory turns
as this ghost comes once again to prowl.
        we reach.
doors move by our grasping fingers
down halls hiding events behind
        intricate keyholes:
slide across brass, bronze quartz
        glass doorknobs.
reflections flicker-thick and thin
from those polished surfaces
        moving beyond marble archways:
monuments of triumphs
      doing something—somewhere.
still, the life curled ice of hate
hurled from darkness, matches a cold
        reflection of mine.
turn, oh turn slowly the identities
        of man-
        the many one-faces
        staring.
you and i, of many one-faces, find a door
and look beyond the glass doorknobs
        to watch our past unfold
        before we breathe it again.
we sleep in the presence of life,
dream of legends that walk hungry hollows
        of mind-
        stalk empty corners
        of destiny
to enter fates repose—shot through with
        brilliantine and
turn, oh so slowly, the many one-faces
      beside endless hallway
        doors.

premonition

a claw ripens within
an icy fist of reality,
lavender nails scrape
secret gashes across the
edge of candle glow.
safety lies in the center
of light—discloses no
open wounds, only a
faintly webbed overlay
of scar tissue, barely
traceable by the heart.

magnolias never blossomed
in the front yard between
tidy hedges, although there
was a proper sort of trellis
covered over with virginia
creeper that housed a
cushioned swing.
the compromise, always obvious
peeks out of dreams
slipped from trunks and
scrapbooks to examine in detail.

the beds we must lie in
are the ones we make,
the mattresses rotting
beneath us that we
may not notice or
replace with new ones
(that's terribly extravagant in
these times of forever famine).
      mirror, mirror in my hall
      cleanse my dreams with alcohol
no image- unwavering
to cling/live up to
only baby's breath
hiding fangs and
lilac bushes covering
scorpion's nests.

cold winters freeze the
corneas of my perception
into stop/go slides,
scenes etched outside
the warm sepia tones of
sunbaked earth.
trumpet vines hang from
a cave filled rock and i
lift them to trace the
lavender scratches
carved in the stone.

echoes

lemonwood and chipped varnish
cradled in your arms now
sing your glad freedom songs.
hollow reed breaths of
eight tone scales echo
your trainless whistle out across
fog bound nights
to walk the trestle of your thoughts
built across silver creek.
i do not know the scent of
cudzu or magnolias-
only the honeysuckle of your
backyard birth is familiar to me.
i do not know the miles
of blacktopped highways
you've walked or the routes
of freights you've hopped-
only an occasional truck stop
night time of your first
wandering is familiar to me.

lemon rinds hover at
the back of my throat.
sea brine to wash my face
stings with the bite of thorns
as i watch the bits of pool tables
at the corners of your mouth—glitter
as i watch the clarity i hugged
so close—disappear.
lemonwood chosen with care
will ripen its tone with age
as my sadness ripens
reaching out to you past
the lemon rinds at the
back of my throat.

crystals from dialogues

1.
i do not sense intimate
touches of reality
from you
but understand the
spider webs you weave;
pepper and salt to
cover tracks released
from clover blossoms.

that falcon hood you wear
to protect your eyes
does not define your politics-
we cannot see who you are.

rumor replaces dialogue;
justifies dogmas
threaded   with thistles
and molded chain-link
blue prints held in trust
by a generation of
longer visions.

i see bricks build stronger places
enclose tools -withhold candles
recover chimney soot
to smear on children's faces

and so mark them
to be remembered
when the last game
of jacks is played-
because the ball was lost.

2.
unleashed amusement parks
invade the upper levels
of disciplined thought.
-get serious   (she cried
the lone ranger is lost
in sherwood forest and the
minataur will devour him
if we don't hurry.
the only animal that knows
he can die is the only
animal that searches for
himself in the outer heavens
and walks down alleys
crunching broken glass
beneath his heels.

-the pool hall has carpet on
the floor, the eight ball is
painted red and my jacks
are rusty   (she mumbled
to nobody in particular
while the fun house lady
laughed her canned laughter
over and over.
there was no one to understand
why the laughing lady died
when the amusement park
on the edge of the ocean
vanished.

3.
lift the octopus.
untangle a herd of whales
to elongate time shards into
pomegranate seeds.
follow thistles across broad
avenues of palm transplanted out
of context, dismissed by cockatoos
and tucans. i miss the warm of
danish featherbeds and the
comfort of retablos on the walls.
bits of before, when marigolds
were bright color - smelled
awful and still do.

-it isn't easy,   (she explained
crowds are such a bother and
streets are nowhere-.
he prefers nowhere, the other
side of planets, anguish or joy
encapsuled into rock candy
to rot teeth in swift silence.
how quiet the night is
beyond the himalayas; within
tabernacles in secret places.
santo niños carved from cottonwood
roots glow aged, paint chipped from
the face of an infanta -lace dress
yellow, dusty and out of season.

elohim-   elohim-
in context, within words chosen to
live centuries and more. a pattern, a
recipe left behind. the continuous thread
from dead centuries. he found that thread.
who he is doesn't matter- but he knows
the recipe by heart.

4.
be still.
winter's night deposits clay
in windy stone hollows where
crooked trees wave withered
leaves outside, whisper
spring's coming and demand
that crickets sing.

that comet
exploded the visions of
star gazers. ripped delicate
fabrics apart and united new
threads of being into multilayered
awe -what happened kohoutek?
where did you go -brimming
dreams into suns loaded with
confiscated future webs?

this darkness
still carries the silence of
tears and gunshot terror.
we speak symbolical concepts
legislated for social order- ignore
the neighbors and procrastinate
our lives for some personal myth
that might guarantee individual rights.

let's pretend
the old order is renovated-
all is well and summer fruit
will ripen as always for harvest.
the gentle sleeps amidst daily
confusions restore hyacinths
and hummingbird wings.
sweet plum blossoms bring
tomorrow on time.

5.
i read somewhere
that kindness
was the beginning
of cruelty
and concubines
were more famous
than wives
and gutenberg
took it all out
of our hands
and created
a **ditto** machine
and 1+1+1 is 3
which is trinity
which is
a symbol used to
explain something
having to do
with a god
who disappeared
because nobody
believed in him
anymore because
he's not really
santa claus and
this is the year
of the kali yuga
and a prayer wheel
makes a lot
of noise
and a love-beast
loves everything
incarnate on earth
and a fool is
a perfect cipher
and **p o e t r y**
was a song
with a story
that was sung
by a blind man
with an ear
for sound

and the nose
of a reporter.
but meter and rhyme
for the lyrics
led to free
interpretation
and too much
imagination
which gave gutenberg
the idea
to present
the facts.

and the new(s)
stories
came out in
black and white
no sound attached
and the bards
went out of business
and **poetry** went into
ditto prison.

and preachers
and teachers
cried -**thou shalt not**
and the machine
roared: **d i t t o**
purred ditto
poured dittoes
into all the hands
in all the lands
and concubines
disappeared
along with empires
and monarchs and
the machine gave birth:
**the evolution of
extension began—**
began—began—began
around in a circle
you fold the
prayer-wheel and

message bringer woman-

you can **read**
about the sound
and the evolution
continues
into revolution
continuously
because:
we all want
our own way.

i read somewhere
that kindness
was the beginning
of **cruelty**.

6.
slip the mickey in the glass
on the line between the dots
watch the dragon lady smile and bring
flashes of distant places while exotic
faces rearrange the time they arrived in.
not the real dragon lady in gold lamé
—haunting smiling jack   -but
a variation on that theme.

in the last row of the balcony he watches—
and thinks about macao and the yakuza
gambling dens as her smooth body
murmurs small movements to the music
and he might have been: john garfield
or clark gable flyin p-38's out of burma
settin down in mindanao or okinawa—to find
the dragon lady lithe and rippling in the
smoky blue secret back rooms
too far removed for him to reach
too dangerous to touch -but his
longing stays there, just the same
undulating in his eyes to the music
to the rhythm—to the madness in his soul
to the rhythm of the music in his mind.

on the line between the dots
on his mind between the spaces
in the movie on the screen—the
dragon lady rapes him with her eyes.
betrayed by his lust, he submits to his
passion and his body writhes with the music
with the look of her etched on his senses
because—he cannot touch her.
the dragon lady is exotic, elusive
and oriental—and he is smiling jack
all american boy.

in transition

this tragedy of words
corners twilight with
deft strokes.
covers sorrow
passing grey impregnated
sleep through early morning
cloud sighs.
wet mountain peaks
clamber into a clutch of sky
stand poised in solemn mists
wait for sunlight to slide
back into the sea.

columns of flame
dance twisted, char fireflies
tilt that essence of purple
cloth caught in balance
between dark and night.
moorish temples relate mosaics
to distance. trumpets call out
the stream of time, echo the
fall of walls—the carpets
shredded, crumbled
beyond repair.

this tragedy of words
cannot disclose: the loss
of arcane majesty;
illusion beyond a now
real or profane; lost shores
of invisible dimensions
uncharted-
          no license to pilot
          no bureau of guidance
          to lift the dawn.

luchar!* to struggle—is the valor
of this untended day.
the sleep of dreamless sleeps
in watchful nights removes
mountains, clears air of wet

salt spray, reclaims gold from
sunstreaked clouds.

to unlock the magic with
rusty keys defies all laws.
even aladdin's accident
was just that.
what treasure hidden
in buffalo hides could
give solace? could replace
the tension of this moment
with something dearer
never sought before?

why question flowers their cause
        for beauty
when candles can wound night's
        embrace.

a robin's color coincides in the
eyes with a morning glory
gravity pulls the tipis down
warriors growl in the throat
        of a fox-
the call is insistent—goatskin drums
beat the measures of the times—
        the time
        this time laden tragedy
        occurs.

[*luchar-to struggle]

yesterday

i can't go there
      anymore
      where
you would have me go.
it's an unfriendly place
peopled with unguarded
thoughts and released
      anger and
i feel uncomfortably un
      civilized somehow.

call, you will
call to remind and
remember those long
lost days spent in wine
to conjure up nothing
to claim we are
whatever it is
we were then-
      hoping none of us
really remembers the
absence of everything
we worked so hard
      to pretend
we didn't want.

some of us
are still there
      pretending.
      some of us
have gone away-
accepting.

street fairs & hierarchies

1.
my god garrity!
this amusement park has
gotten out of hand!
i can't stop the cannibals
from going at it—but i do
think we can slow the pace.

> mime the rhyme
> in frequent spaces
> conjure up
> the boney ash-
> the brain **will** will
> what has been
> put upon it.

stand up i say!
and speak your moment
this monumental effervescence
complains the gnashes in my ear
trip easy to the vortex
hold steady in the eye
then cast the whale
from lochinvar
window jumping clever cleavers
in my mind.

> quote by rote
> the assignation-
> some simple
> commentary
> of the hour.

2.
mildew edges
bricked walks
on faces bobbing
light ahead
typewriter clacking monster
knocks up the words
swollen, fattened

on the page-
won't rot in warmer weather
crawling back to
bed the lights, the
faces molding in
the sea.

3.
calamity jane & two gun lil
see-saw the daw
up and down the count
to ten and up again
the bloody west
is gone—the gun
guns here guns here

crackerjack prizes
and tin badges
conduct all the parades
in the squares and
i salute you
i salute you.

4.
come back
the morning of mourning
and count the notches on
the hanging trees swinging there
machine gun tatooed-
roses on the markers:
broken teeth and dented skulls
to tell us who we are

headline photographs daily news
poignant etching count
down the moon
to tell us who we are.
museums bulging fatted
for the feast
we've come to town
we're on display
come!   —tell us who we are!

5.
misa de los ángeles*
mixed meditations of the saints
litanies of language
tumble from my tongue
cantos—encantos
enchanted mysteries
misteriosos lugares
disappear into folklore
myths and theologies
come back to haunt
the dead and
here we are:
resurrecting all we were.

6.
cayuga falls
sky blue sequin splattered
coats of arms
b i a numbers richly
embroided or beaded
on tribal crests-
clan symbols and mottoes
reverently displayed proof
of lineage **and** ancestry-
                    damn it euphemia!
                    what have we come to?

and you know it will happen
will happen in that way.

7.
burbons, tudors,
plantagenets, stuarts
sitting bulls, tecumsehs,
josephs, geronimos
villas, castros
allendes, gueverras
these chromosomal threads
stretching into
future centuries-
spectacular genealogies
coming together:

royal crossbreeds of
miscegenation
producing pedigrees of
genetic content
documentation of
affiliation and education to:

        tell us who we are
        tell us **w h o** we are.

[*misa de los ángeles: mass of the angels;
cantos: songs;
encantos: enchantments;
misteriosos lugares: mysterious places.]

yo quiero cantar*

yo quiero cantar
because life is so fine
from my eyes
yo quiero gritar
ándale! come on!
vamos a bailar:
no te entiendes
ni comprendes
ni sabes
whatever it is
you're saying
let's dance hombre!
all that retention is
gonna explode you
por cierto / for sure.
loosen up your
s a c r o i l i a c
gyrate your pelvis
hey!
ándale ándale
vamos a bailar
con una índia
con una árabe
con una gringa
una mestiza-
mama gonna mam **bo**
with you
gonna sam **ba**
and mer rin **gue**
and pa chan **ga**
hey!
mix it up
and hold on tight

gentleman jim
smokes a big fat cigar
tips his panama to the folks
taps his cane upon the floor
by gosh, by jingo
by golly, by gee

got a hair transplant
got a heart transplant
got a kidney transplant
got a new set of teeth
and is waitin for his eyes
alley oop vanity
mix it up and
hold on tight.

yo quiero cantar
because life is so fine
from my eyes
yo quiero cantar
que te amo
pero no puedo
i can't si te hablas
talk too much
mira como eres!

lady jane
don't wear no bra
don't wear no satin
don't wear no lace
don't wear no make-up
don't curl her hair
hmm uhhh hmm ummh
wears faded clothes
all washed out blue
don't smoke cigarettes
'cause it ain't cool
she studies yoga
and aikido and
drinks an awful **lot**
of tea-
ma ma git **d o w n**
and **sing** with me
mix it up and
hold on tight.

yo quiero cantar
because life is so fine
from my eyes
through mis espejos rosas

y yo quiero a bailar contigo
quieres a bailar conmigo?
con una mestiza?
bueno pues-
yo quiero cantar
because life is so fine
porque la vida
is so fine
porque la vida
is so fine
y yo quiero a
cantarle a **ti!**

[*yo quiero cantar: i want to sing;
yo quiero gritar: i want to shout;
ándale: come on;
vamos a bailar: let's dance;
no te entiendes: i don't understand you;
ni compredes: nor comprehend you;
ni sabes: nor know;
hombre: man;
por cierto: for sure;
con una índia: with an indian;
árabe: arab;
gringa: foreigner;
mambo, samba, meringue, pachanga: the names of various latin dances;
que te amo: that i love you;
pero, no puedo: but, i can't;
si te hablas: if you talk;
mira como eres: see how you are;
mis espejos rosas: my rose (colored) glasses;.
y yo quiero bailar contigo: and i want to dance with you;
conmigo: with me;
con una mestiza: with a mixed blood;
porque: because;
la vida: (the) life;
y yo quiero a cantarle a ti: and i want to sing of it to you.]

the exiles

it was the bright lite fever
            got us all
gettin away from podunk towns
all over nowhere boonies usa-
            (let's make it man!
            check out the scene-
sluggin jukeboxes in low life dives
south edith north fourth south first
curtis broadway mission olvera main
bobby sox sweater girls hanging out every night
lookin for fun and fast rides downtown with
ducktail boys in jeans wearin loafers or wingtips
to the movies -for a hamburger -for a beer
            -for a goodtime -anytime.
                        moths headin for neon
                        phosphorescent glow
                        sending signals thru the dark
                        special message -flashin codes
                        flashin the good life
                        green and red
                        buildin the longin
            -for that alltime -goodtime -high!

wakin up head bangin stale beer
cigarette butts city carbon city noise
bad taste mouth blood shot eyes
puke on the floor wadin thru a fuckin mess
tryin to remember:

                        the smell of the lookin
                        early evenin cruisin
                        the smell of the waitin
                        the first bottle of beer
                        the smell of adventure
                        the packards the hudsons
                        the buick convertibles
                        the smell of the neon night
                        (let it all hang out
                        the call of the neon lite!

walkin robot thru endless days
ugly -frumpy -city days
cold or hot   wet or dry
window shoppin grocery buyin
draggin thru countless daylite daze
   -late afternoon longin
     in the pit of the stomach
watchin twilight soften the city
    waitin for it to happen again
the taste -the smell   -the feel of the **night!**

   lady night!
   covered in sequins
   lady night!
   dressed in her finest
   lady night!
   filled with music and
   dancin and
   movement everywhere!
   lady night!
   exotic and beckonin
touchin us all with the bright lite fever
catchin us forever with the neon glow
attachin our souls to the nighttime longin
endlessly searchin the big city streets for:
   -that alltime -goodtime   -high!

2.
back home
small town scene
big city scramble far behind
drenched with quiet -save a gust of
wind -cicadas hum   -bull frog'
songs and cricket's chatter
days sparklin bright with
monotonous routine
clear nights showin off
every star
moonlite paths crisscrossing fields
a coyote call
a hoot owl whirr

easy livin
slow days   -long nights
reservations dusty and still
small town stores gather the folks
to share the news -buy staples or
a luxury or two-
back home   -quiet and easy

       horses for herdin
       trucks for haulin
       ditches to clear
       corn to plant
       beans to plant
       squash to plant
       prayin
       prayin the rain
       singin the rain
       dancin the rain
each day's twilight hushes chickens and dogs
scampers children inside for the evenin meal
banks the fires   -ends the chores.

easy livin won't smother the longin
soft nights don't cover that feelin
clean air won't hide:
       the smell of the lookin
     . the smell of the waitin
       knowin it's out there
       it's out there -somewhere
the taste   -the smell -the feel of the night!

goin up the road
       -moon ridin high
to have a beer - hear a song
goin up the road to a
one horse bar
       in a podunk town
       no neon glow
       no convertible shine
no goodtime gang to make the scene
knowin we're all doin time!
just doin our time whether
it's inside or out-

check you later baby!
-don't sweat me man
got to get outta here-
got to click on **cee**-ment
on sidewalk **cee**-ment
got to find me a honky tonk bar
on a big city street-
got the bright lite fever
burnin my soul
got to find me

-that alltime   -goodtime   -high!

the cry

somber greens dissolve into forest twilights
to vanish through a tangled network canopy
unable to hold the day's reflections.
one last point of reference disintegrates as
fog closes in—shutting out the marble balustrade
hanging there, in that slice of sky.

> on to nottingham then-
> there are choices to
> be made.

random harmonies pierce layers
of muffled grey gauze—tracing patterns
of a solitary star.
triads spinning from quadrants
describe in chromatics—the arc of that star
flares brilliant prismatic geometries
leaving an indigo flecked cobalt stain
as indelible after image.
madness creeps through layers of
sensitivity to determine these variables
of selection.

> why have you defined
> the dimensions of
> our loneliness?
> what consequence of love
> is that?

our madness lies in synapse jumps
exploding circuits printed with too much feeling.
interrupted currents nudge unconscious
commands and new connections overload
with confusion.

> what consequence to
> be more alone than before?
> enclosed within the shell
> of no escape
> each confined to consciousness

forever destined to reach for
a freedom that does not
exist for us now.

tonal octads writhe in diminished forms-
coalesce to bridge the gaps of disorientation
born in madness.   chaos is humane.
it restores clarity. resumes the natural
order of things.

it is the wounds
that demand careful attention
-of these
the poet's speech is made.

knowing that is not knowledge
not yet aware of suffering-
lurks in memories
lays constricted in the back of
the throat—wanting to be released
into the sustained cry of human agony
while gods dream of mortal death
asleep in immortality.

what skill to lace the
branches of forest trees
with morning gold and
scatter the honeysuckle bush
with hummingbirds' wings.

what torment to understand the integration
of dying and the destruction of unity—in living.
it is written in the fabric of the cosmos that:
earth is the borning place of individuation.
overlay that with the will to survive and
individuality as treasure above all things.

what skill to transmute ecstasy
into terror of unknown spheres
and spice it with longing for
forgotten things.
do you remember the
first crystal you formed

before you were made to forget
the songs of nebulae?

a field of ebony flushed with crimson
descends to cover faint trails into memory
spreads new longings—blanket warm on
nerve endings. in my dreaming i know
it is my love for you.

what death to choose
beyond random multiple choices?
what chord to strike
above the madness
when dying comes?

nottingham is no more.
it lies buried in the dust of legend
forgotten why it was
along with robin hood's forest.

crushed rose petals drift along the
edges of loneliness. the hushed fragrance
climbs twilight's softened hues   reaching
for one small slice of cobalt sky.

somewhere
there sits a sea of the same color
surrounding an island of
polished indigo that holds my
reflection in the very center.

why do i see you standing on a marble balcony?
a shard of some forgotten-time-fragmented-
vision-of-somewhere left within you and
the scent of cinnamon oil and
damascus on the night.
a muezzin call lingers on the east wind.
one note fading into baked mosiac tiles-
that color you carry as identity.

i define my choice.
all my skies are cobalt
and i know

message bringer woman-

roses must bear thorns.

one note swells into an agonized cry-
one opalescent tear drop hurled
into the universe from
shattered   silence.

sing aleph-
aleph is the beginning again.

through the microscope series

1.
the lesson of tigers
has something to do
with stripes and
the changing
of them
clawed to ribbons
you will remember
with indelible accuracy
the moment of attack

cat silent
the leap   -the strike
no warning is
ever issued by
the jungle variety

the mountain bobcat
displays some integrity
growls deep in the throat
just before it pounces
on its prey

the lesson of leopards
and lynxes and cheetahs
relates to their spots

of lions and jaguars and
panthers the law of the
jungle holds true
no warning—cat silent
the leap   the strike-
and oftentimes
the kill!

2.
he looked into the eye of sodom
poised -settled   -blinked twice and
disappeared sand castles and moon rivers.

watch my hair darken   (he sd
and i thought to wonder when i'd
last seen gold pillow strands.

those eagle feathers
touched with cloud and sunset
send many years of learning
to echo quiet sighs
through necklace bones.
        my hands wither-
        look like grandma's
        thin and veined.
        the hands mark
        the journeys-
        do not lie.

this presence is detached with no
motion inside the dust devil
only the edges whirl and glitter as
i move away from all i have known.
        we are not alike anymore
        (you and i
        nor of that time-
        i have separated
        into other places and
        persons of me.

i watch dominos slide
across sandstone table tops
count five multiplied as
square roots tumble in
geometric progressions and
i am free-
i have found the curve
of my own space.

sentinels hold watch in that land
will secure what they must and

100

leave the winds hold sway
over the rest.
return then   -and mourn
what cannot be stopped
(my hands flung helplessly skyward
sell it to a dustbowl!
cíbola will be raped once more
pieced and parceled -grain by grain
drained of her blood **by her own**.

        my hands look like grandma's tonight
        old   -wrinkled and worked
        like grandma's when she
        was old and remembered
        early morning bathing
        in the river   -when she was a girl.
        strong hands   -marked with
        journeys never told.

3.
satisfy this midnight closing
itself to linear realities.

        snow fell somewhere else
        but i felt the cold clear night
        soft with flakes and
        deep with winter.

from the north: geese move in formation.
dark angles against grey skies come south
to bring us the message of snow.
two swans come first, descending from the north

holding plumes and prayers skyward
shifting into a probable future   -now.

        i send messages to god
        in stamped self addressed envelopes
        backwards through time and
        ask questions about 30th
        century manuscripts   -ask why
        today is tomorrow turned
        inside out.

all time coincides in brilliant points of light
two sparrows come close to
peek at the realm of captivity
inspect cages and forms-
everyone in sight becomes warden or guard
friend or benefactor

> freedom spans consciousness
> telescopes realities
> carries notes and syllables
> -from snowflakes.

atoms cry and a comet flies south for the winter.

4.
provocative moments of
magnificent splendor
                    intoxicate me
'telekinetic cholinergia'
                    after the dance

dance the muscles
drum the beating drum
chant the sutras
8 to 14 cycles per second
there is a reason—there is a reason
alpha rhythms correspond—but
the magic subsides
                    even in siberia
                    even in tibet.

beat the drum
dance the dance or
hold the breath
you will discover
the result is the same-
there is a reason to:
                    know thyself
                    -as   (he sd

5.
-grandfather's comin back
one of these days   (he sd
and tears sprang to my eyes
i couldn't stop
            (but in the meantime
we just have to be ordinary
trapped humans and
            i resent that!

third planet from the sun
movin in
grandfather's comin back
to check us out
see if we made it and how and
            (i sd
they don't even understand
the meaning of coyote.

all things are only symbols.
that eagle feather represents:
            did you hear what i sd?
is a connecting point
a synapse jump to that other
place we have forgotten about.

this place is in-between
a backwards way of going home
like coyote playin tricks again
and hidin in the drum.

they understand their jung—and
long to hold their dreams awake
but cannot see relationships of:
                        bone to feather
                        breath to wind
                        sun to spirit
                        earth to mother
                        rock to sand
coyote laughin all the time
disappearin into the desert to
consult the badger twins
old spider woman noddin wise-

these reminders
all around us
that grandfather's comin back one day
to tell us another dream
to call the wind and lift the sun
and shift the morning star
while old coyote laughs the moon away
and maybe—if we remember those
long ago dreams
he'll tell us
why
we are.

6.
side slips
into books of myselves.
these lives i document as
time strung mattered molecules
(who holds this head
in agony today?
what battle—where?
woke us uneasy—here?
how many simultaneous
meeting places
pulse in and out?

we won—here
(for a space of moments
did loss occur—some other place?

weary ache through hot days
bits of air hang oppressive
you joust in heat waves.

easy explanations filter close
just outside my line of sight.

slide slips
into parallels-
the countess leaped centuries
to whisper secrets in a language
unknown to me.

a courtesan, i understood-
sought after in her day from
york to pembroke
through parlours and county fairs
        then side slip
        and back here.

7.
this house of cards falls up
with eight bells on the path
i come to live a -lone -to -gether.

five years sideways
i found the thread
that place conjured
to be now:
        warm hearth—warm home.

that tone so clear in moment change
will leap my neurons here to
there and fire forward once again:
        eight bells behind my head
        i see my coming to   -gether
        to   -gather
        in this to   -day.

8.
what will-o-the-wisp of scattered field
what half life radiation point can
name the pose—the congruent change
inherent in any probable choice?

this **be**
i will   and
am   **become**
from selective acts of
cooperative struggle
        (each atom so designed
can choose to agree.

what is the place we congregate?
this space we call around us?
this time we inflict upon ourselves?
                    i elude the space i inhabit.

9.
sombre lustre augers yestermorrows
nowwhens in some other tense-
                    future present
                    past perfect
this citadel will satisfy no quantum.

dig me out of this neuron lapse
too fast for me to calculate the
why of anything.
to sense the future in cellular fashion
with no reason to hang these emotions on
this dire foreboding a time locked tense
                    a warning bell shudder
                    through the fiber of my being
is a body vaccine
to minimize that trauma that
waits to be.

10.
i go now
and so i go.
let them go
go to yestermorrows
day to days

i bid my dreams
maybe remember
who i must which you i found
which dream came here
what now i sleep and
wake myself
a   -lone   to   -gether
to   -gather me
from you.

11.
and lone—ly
will not be
my place or time.

inventing stars is
what i do
and hunting lions
to talk about-
and mountain goats
to share those peaks
of dimension leaps

and lone—ly
will not
be
in me.

whistle stops

—about whistle stops—

this cycle of poems came into being between 1976 and 1978—
first as notes, thoughts and images about the people, places and events
that i experienced while i was statewide coordinator for the california
poets in the schools program then became poems. during those two
years, i not only traveled extensively throughout the state staying for one
or two nights in each new place in strange motel rooms or with people
i'd just met, i also discovered a california i didn't know through the
voices of her poets—region by region. it was an exciting and a difficult
time and i still view those years as the most significant period of my life
because i learned so much from so many people. whistle stops reflects
what i was experiencing as i drove or flew to meetings, seminars,
workshops in many different communities speaking to parents, teachers,
local business organizations and arts councils about living poets who
love language and make poems.

whistle stops is my love song to california and her 'pits' poets
and it belongs to them. So does my grateful acknowledgement and
deepest thanks to the following people. first to leonard randolph
(wherever he is), former nea literature director, who 'planted' the pits
programs in all fifty states because he believed that real poets in the
classrooms of america would share their love for language with young
people and create future generations of readers who would understand
and appreciate 'living' american poets as well as dead ones; to francis
gretton and floyd salas who recruited me; to office staff poets eileen
malone and bernie gershenson who handled so much so well and to all
my fellow poets out there wherever you are— thank you ben hiatt, james
krusoe, john oliver simon, devorah major, shelley savrin, mary norbert
korte, will staple, bill howarth, john allen cann, susan beersworth, kit
robinson, bill berkson, jack grapes, sharon cheedle, tobey kaplan, pat
parker, harold littlebird, bob gallegher, wanda coleman, steve sanfield,
xelina, alurista, lane nishikawa, luis sequiya, duane bigeagle, dale
pendell, roz spafford, javier pacheco, wendy rose, barrett watten, paula
rath, george leong and poets i neglected to mention, for going into so
many classrooms. it is with much affection that i dedicate these poems,
this love song— to all of you.

venice beach

what night this romance in
fantasy foiled
this galahad droll and
tingling with suspense.
clusters of words loom
mysterious
eyes look away carefully
to notice not seeing.

avalon sits offshore out there-
an isle of songed romance
glass bottomed boats
and music.
a legend many times retold
and i don't even know if
it's still there
like i don't know who
you are in this background-
this place **you** call home.

that death should enter into
these preoccupations-
these modes of function
that tell us life **is**
is around every corner
we meet:
congruent moment points
intersect-
these things happen only
when they can. . . . .

suppose yesterday had not-
which maybe
spider-spun across lines
of connections would have
taken place?
we knew outside ourselves
this now would come to be.

raw-boned is the phrase that
best describes the whole of you
but with such graceful
delivery of motion.

don't rush. oh no.
don't complicate the crystal
so fragile
waiting there.
birds flutter close
in hesitation
falter in the moment.
don't hurry quiet adventure
let it build slow motion
watch it grow.

santa monica

tides turn into
no sunset tonight
my too fast pace
doesn't match any
movement around me
i forgot those ways
displaced them
in some other time.

out of context this mood-
a different reality
these reflections of symbols
from another place
his table banging fist
slides off into silence
ends our dinner conversation
reminds me of
my father growing old.

i want to ask so many
unimportant questions
i want to talk nonsense
because serious considerations
about anything fade in and out
yes: out of sync
like thomas paine on education
and shelly's ode filled with
sonnets but
no matter how it went.

san francisco

triptichs settle in my mind
you me **you**
you me him
you me her
you you you
us we they

i carry these motífs around
not connected   yet
interlocked inside me.
we will remain unidentifiable
on the whole
you must decide
which **you**
which her
which him
which me
lies trapped upon the page
unnamed
unspecified
indistinguishable
from all the rest.

so many lives seep through
my bones
and as many faces

slide past my eyes
unmarked

i will reproduce the
meanings i derived
those whens
upon these pages for
you   to think about.

you   do not answer my calls
cannot receive communication
from this mythical land.
a disconnection of some sort
yet i respond to **your** insistence
and you are not there to
answer **your** need for me.

you   glow somehow
wrapped in secret tragedies
holding court in private
just after we'd sd
suffering was not good
for the soul.

i remembered myself
watching those created
attractions i once gathered
round me and saw the distance
i've moved toward
new beginnings
new forms and shapes to
symbolize my universe.

los angeles county

south winds harbor warmth
and gentle kind
the king of the south is
made of these things.
of north wind it is sd

there is strength and power
the harsh sting of frost.

these gifts brought forward
meet in west wind
face east toward
grandfather
giver of all things
home of eagle and sun.

how high the eagle flies
to view the whole.
scaled in miniature-
this perspective is lost
by the scorpion
hidden beneath rocks.

santa monica canyon

crickets sing in this
quiet valley where
i take my sleep and
i find myself waiting for
foghorns to warn the night
they are there.

i take **you** into my memory
carry **you** outside this time
into other realms i know
only in dreams.
this form **you** say
is immortality!

you sit in the hollow
of my breath
luxuriant dew and sea salt
languish on my tongue.

that **your** vision is close
and wants only fat letters
to lick from books
plays tricks with
spatial moods and
tense declensions.

sacramento

my contention good sir!
is to note the nascent
diversion of any mind into
moments of alternate fields
those other places where
one might focus contentedly.

the sensation notwithstanding the
pulse of the time causes argument
out of all proportion to being.

contrived   you say? so be it
discoursed among us then.
taxidermy is not my favorite sport
though i can stuff "stuff" with
the best of them

folsom/marysville

my inspiration flows deftly
through these whistle stops
upon the page
these talking leaves of lives
there on oaks
above american river
among doorknobs and windowsills
and photographs of places been

then down the road
to a private place
back door river and elm tree shade
for ten speed bikes
eight track tapes
sixteen millimeter flickers into
fun or another way of looking

are **you** ever quiet? (he asked
and i was glad my rainbow was
still bright upon the canvas
on his wall.

sentiment runs through woods
and under palms
you   build my legend warm and far

you   call me my lady
light my cigarettes and i
allow myself to say today-
long live the queen!

san francisco

log jammed days tumble
season changed through
winter pushing south-
long distance between us.

funny words say themselves
as i watch your lips
single out the spaces
wrapped in exploration
around deeper tones not
uttered yet.

the sun balled cherry red on
lake merced to explain the
day's intense heat
suspended-

mine waits to be dropped
to cool
drained off in
small degrees.

-oh the shark has -
but he forgot to say
how many anythings
had passed him by.

rancho cordova

he   wanted to know what
i did with power
(making fists in the air
while overwhelming himself
with his overwhelming view
of who he   was.

locate barriers and
knock them down! (i sd
they're only ninepins
in a row
five'll getcha ten
we all come out even

-and   **you** with moonrocked arms
will not touch me while   **you**
carry another's voice
in   **your** mouth-

i play with it! (i sd
and we laughed the world
into many corners
watching shadows break
morning roosters into song.

asilomar

i cannot possibly absorb
every word ever written-
defend my life with
quotation marks-
my livelihood with litanies
of sainted lives-

those bones gone down
in printer's ink.

sometimes
i envy the suicide of
black roses and mermaids
the provocative agony of
vivisection
the sweet clutching fear
of letting go-
though fascination with
the scythe can clutter
cloudy days.

santa monica

there's the chemistry of it
to consider   (**you** sd
that no-stop-want that
happens just like that
i know that instant   (i sd
tracing sandstone and
a girl boy memory back
to electric sixteen and
a cool cave under 'dead man's
corner' in tijeras canyon where
our mouth's connected to make
the current flow-
we only held each other

didn't break the spell and
i never saw him again.

you   offer whiskey breath
a glass of wine and
an ocean view
while I mumble -nice place-
wine is the discoverer of secrets
(confucius say
or the other side of the coin
not shown   (i sd
the fashionable moment of
the easy lay subdues these
careful courtships
runs them underground to
surface again when better
times come round.
annex my propriety if **you** will
it bothers me to know
my chemistry
is missing **yours**.

san francisco/oakland

violins for breakfast
a real quartet and a balcony
dressed in palmed sunshine-
an outside dream of
a time to come
where   **your** shadow hovers
in morning dew.

i will organize certain syllables
into sound patterns
tonals that <u>do</u>
instead of represent (re / present
and i will call   **you**

up out of darkness
and memory
with the drum beat
of my blood and
we will dance on our
thoughts set in motion
with breath from
our hearts.

american river

latter days number us
side by side
locked in center folds
of our own lives

no time waits everywhere
precludes action/reaction
and i create crickets tonight
along with frogs to accompany
a tchaikovsky concerto
on the hi-fi.

there's no tv here   (he sd
but i didn't mind moving
myself through mountains
to pen and page.

vallejo

'juju call the bone man
he come lookin over
the shoulder
make everything dark'

leaving me on the front steps
staring at a star
running rainbows
just for me

on the road to
nut tree stop
heading home
thinking years of plotting
freedom from traps and fences

how odd to see the fences
i've built and why
i kept them as
justifiable monuments to:
ought tos.

san diego/el cajon

'and juju conjur music night
dispense the jugglers
rev up the brain
wash away the sins of matter'

don't deify   **your** love (he sd
mythological name dropping
hides what's going on

now the shark has. . .
a knife man
getting sharp inside the game
linguistics for a whet stone
semiotics for the oil.

the ace of hearts
will cop a plea and
tijuana del sur
caminando al norte
comiendo la gente

y en 'los' no hay
hermanos escritores.

teeth are flourescent white
under black light.

la jolla

a buddhist existentialist is?
a zen fascist with a cover story
(he sd
but the liberal in the background
wasn't paying any attention.

this is where i'm at
this is where i'm at
this is where i'm at
(he sd

whenever we reach this
moment point
coincidence scatters mercury
and satire well beyond
any definable boundaries-

you'll never move the masses
if **you** can't stir the sauce
(he sd

and don't use small plates-
they don't hold enough
of anything.

san francisco

'juju bent the whistle
fore he could call
changed his mind
a dozen times
mixed and matched!'

art does not exist to make
your living   (the artist sd
but the collector went on
collecting everything in sight
his fat pocketbook loudly
denouncing the right of
painters to resale royalties.

it's confiscation of property!
(the collector sd
<u>my</u> property   **now**!

manhood is the pride of:
sanctuary in mid-stream
savings accounts in
world banks of
warn out dreams
pensive moments and
tarnished silver.

cotati/rohnert park

morning on dusty roads
brings past/futures
into view
coincides with that other
new mexico morning
i did not live.
this now
this me
posited in

rural california-
new mexico somewhere
behind me

moves toward
different conclusions
because
i'm not there
anymore.

salinas to santa barbara

driving alone down
the palm strewn
one-oh-one-
loving every wind
designed cypress
hugging coastal bluffs
and rocky points-
a 1930's new mexico
childhood memory
coincides with this landscape:

(uncle john sd
-brother bob went on
to the promised land.
didn't like it here.
too dry. too cold. too
dusty. too damn hard.
not for him. wrote us
often enough (sd
-californy's got everything-
got everything anyone
could ever want.

the names of centuries
settle in the laps of
gentle hills cuddled
beneath eucalyptus stands
scrub oak and russian olive groves.

the oil rigs offshore
bite deeply into
grandmother's flesh
bleed her
drop by precious drop
into crisis
and on the allegheny star route
a meditation moves forward

an old idea-
encouraged into being
by forces beyond the ken
of these intimate connections.

we are brought together
uniquely -one at a time-
running down the beach
a mile a day in response
to someone's vague knock.

a tap from a new direction.
no cause and effect here
only changes that rediscover
new options—spread out
in neat array.

palo alto/menlo park

it was the lip-smacking
internal rhyme he fell upon
with surprise in
his intonation of:
quite nice-
that raised the heavy
eyebrows across the room.
another point for:
golden-hair-going-bald
(i thought

the beginnings of another
sensible farce
we will all be forced
to consume at random—
thigh pulls and all.

'and juju drop
the night cold
tumble diamonds
through his eyes
drummin jungles
from the lips of shamans.'

san luis obispo/halcyon

halcyon dune-ites
cluster in seclusion
retold in human interest
as they 'cull cannery bins
for subsistence'
and we marvel at
the freedom they parade
in our heat stained
over crowded minds.

nobody bothered about
them much (she sd
under thunderheads gathered
over san luis plaza
to dramatize that remembered
depressed time etched
deeply in her face.

and this day is censored.
forgotten into that
past / future   '
present! right here
right now!

melrose ave/los angeles

in ventura
the bar bars justice.
blindfolded and gagged
makes up new rules
(without consent
for somebody's glory road.

skyhorse. mohawk.
camisa colorado.
interwoven identities
signify a symbol
we forgot to notice.
swift. swift.
an arrow flies
true aim. the heart
leaps -any day now
the trigger:
watch it s que ee eez ze
sn a p   **fire**
it goes on
in the rubber hose cell
not here. but there.
it goes on and on
over there
in those places
gunned from the rock.
beast caves. over there
in suit and tie
over there
in uniform
not here
(on melrose avenue
where crystal chips
light prayer sticks.

chico/paradise

it surprises the adequate
to: discover holes
in highways of thought.

paradise -
drawn and quartered
bottled for re-sale:
filled with
conversations taking
unexpected turns or
making ill timed stops.

and
juju name : names
i name : myself
call midnight into
whistles-stops;
koshare clowns to dance.

little is the place
i walk about.
a name related
to town and square
translated back to: small
he sd a kaleidescope
of lipbitten words
over yellow flowers
and broccoli and
fall struck leaves
cascading onto streets.

quiet. northcentral.
small. this place
i fly away from.

central coast/morro bay

(he sd
i could take
the cockcrow rooster
to break
the morning with
or dream long afternoons
of dorothy taking
gorceries to the
dune-ites of oceana
back in the 30's
and the 40's
and the 50's-
calling 'the coast guards'
her boys
on spaghetti dinner nights
at her home.

stockton

late louie quinz
flocked blue
and green walls
crowd the meeting moments
in my mind.
this valley claims
tranquility as its base.

sentiment mixed with chopin
sheds light on barriers
and borders.

never break the promise of
a lady love ignored

sentimental shrapnel
will remind you
of transgression.

'and juju hold the light
inside the moon
call heaven: just
another place to
think about'

russian river

and in the summer of
my dream
i find new places i
was not looking for.

that love and
the death of it
should coincide is
not a discovery i
wanted to make-
nor am i certain
it belongs to any of us.

as i watch the movies
of **you** and me-
the missing parts
remain a puzzle
to be solved.

off camera
out of the room
not in the scene
i'm in-
i don't know
who **you** are or
where **you** go.

san francisco

sold out!
and i am bizarre (she sd
two years
coming not home-
but- to where she started
to become sane.   in
spite of: the pain of:
living it like it was.

and **you**
spent tears and anger
at the door because
the tickets were
invisible and could not
be exchanged for
a curtain call.

'and juju pledge equality.
find funny thing on
doorstep - everyday'

marin county

they-
section their lives
into contrasts
expect to compose
each compartment
forever
cross-referenced as:
father: mother:
daughter: son:
brother: sister:
and over again.

we-
gather nightlife in

our eyes and scatter
it to the wild winds;
reclaim our destinies
each solstice we pass.

our-
futures mined with
savage detail
surrogate headhunters
caught in molecules of
turtle island
drums still beat
the ancient rhythms
point -counterpoint

my blood sings
approaching zero.

los angeles

the l.a. pottery party spoke
a different language.
discussed: the dance.
the wheel. music. and-
various accidents of:
memberships-at-large.

a moistened moment
held the stage
toasted a loving union
into welded future fortune.

i am a jewess—(she sd
and i fucking love the south!

and **you** backed unto
judo mats withheld the
kiaaiii of **your** blow and
exhaled harmless banter
instead.

san francisco

look how white it is (he sd
and watched decay mumble
along the edges of another
dimension-
not this one
where polar bears
are held up to the sun
in admiration of their
rainbow effect.

he swallowed a handful
of mexican jumping beans
and landed on his feet.

my my (she sd
do you imagine you'll
grow any more than that?

these movements jostle-
condense sensations into
tight balls of meaning
unwilling to be unraveled
at length.

contra costa

parsnips & rutabagas
10¢ a lb
hawk a rabbit
in the park
converge on dialect
dis mantle ray guns
piece by piece.

surveyors stalk the
midnight land
backbiting infighting

20¢ a shot
ducks on target
bulls eyes—marked
win: a kewpie! or a
plot! at the end of
every game.

raise the flag!
slay the slayer!
freedom's gone beserk
and blake named
the devourers of words!

alameda

the monument of crystal
is: immeasurable.
obsidian knives
left behind to remind of
what was —yet
this volcanic crystal
will disintegrate
in time—over time
will leave no
measurable trace.

she wore mountains
on her shoulders
bending at the waist
to dip water from
the mountain well.
thunder streaked
her hair blue
and black with
momentary clashes.
sunset rode her lips
with envy
for cascading rain
from clouded eyes
across the room.

riverside

santana morning across
forty mile an hour highway
push into the cut
10 minutes late to hear
domingo / laguna / poet / singer
tell of pueblo ways.
he reminds the kids at
sherman school of
special things like:

the indian way of
greeting life.

*   *   *   *   *

time is a frame.
a frame around pictures
we move through.

the buffalo await us in
the magellanic clouds
see: yellow arrow for buffalo
see: yellow buffalo.

and i will dream **you**
into days to come.

napa valley

you
wander gypsy
through my dreams
steal a kiss
strike a bargain
disappear into morning.

a feather floats near
comes to rest
at my feet.
i discover
what i am to do
with these symbols
that i find.

soon
i will weave
them together and
plant them in
the sky.

*   *   *   *   *

i will call **you** beloved
when: the suns dance
red against purple clouds.

san juan county

wind spirits
do not whisper
during the cracking
ice.
no
feather messages
float nearby.

*   *   *   *   *

concentrate on concrete.

consider the magnitude of
gluing sand and pebbles
together in order to:
circumvent
hewing granite from

mountainsides to
build temples in
the valley below.

oh -my relations.

what partial roads we
walk upon.

the long road moves
from east to west
and ends in the house of
the sun.

california

-in the valley of the blind
the hand symbols of the deaf
communicate to no one.

-in the village of the deaf
the language of the blind
makes no sense.

-in the city of the mute
neither blind nor deaf
will understand the
lack of response

when we are all
equally blind deaf
and mute
perhaps we will seek
new ways to make sense of
and understand each other's
languages.

from **excerpts from**
mountain climber's handbook

from crystal

whole bread and milk become meals
sprinkled with clarity and mirth.

what is this sudden need to share the superb
dance of bubbles, whalespouts, rain forests and deserts?
cells and splendor should not combine to
grow such fire between us.

a bass horn and a thrush begin the night here.
i have dreamed your name and heard a
fragment of your song.

there is a tear
hidden in a faraway thought-
a night once dreamed and disappeared.
what futures do we initiate or compromise?
which self occupies these moments we converge our
histories into a common memory?
-is this immortality then?

i chose cobalt skies to carry my reflections,
roses with thorns as life and music and love,
this future / present
already marked in my past.
i was not looking for this connection
between   -this now
when i dreamed you   as you are.

song of the four winds

to inspire a careful language
cautious for other centuries-
we summon
these portfolios out of ourselves.

around us
the halls are crowded with name tags
immortalized in
gold leaf and celluloid
everywhere.

we-
document the quiet change,
walk the edge of the unknown
planting specks of light to note
our discoveries.

the most useable path through oblivion
will bear the mark of
the careful explorers
we've become.

we-
will continue to prosper here,
unnoticed for awhile until
all the webs are untangled

and they will find us-
holding the ends of these threads
a smile caught between us.

this is my body

this is my body
to have and to hold-
to infect   pollute   humiliate
wound   cleanse   contaminate
addict   -or not.

this is my body
to have and to hold-
to fatten   reduce   girdle
show off   hide   pamper
batter   -or deny

this is my hair
to cut   to dye   to streak
to bleach   to kink   to straighten
to grow as i please

this is my face
to stain   to powder   to paint
my nose   my eyes   my lips
my ears   my cheeks   my chin
to scrub   oil   cream   pluck
pierce and shave   to remove
wrinkles and pouches from
or leave to weather and age

these are my breasts
to give and to take away
to nourish my babies by giving
to feed my vanity by not giving
to up lift   or let sag
to enlarge   or remove
they belong to no one
-but me

this is my body
to have and to hold-
my temple
my domain
to do with as i will

to inhabit or cast aside
if i so choose

my body my temple
my domain
not ever to be ordered
or disposed of
by church or state
without my knowledge
without my consent

no black robed justice or judge
no white robed pontif or priest
can claim legal or moral right
in true conscience
to dictate the use of my body
by me

you: fathers   brothers and sons
who unjustly legislate
the use of my womb
then hide behind the law
to subjugate my body
to your will and desire-
you: threaten my life
every minute of
every day in the
name of your male god and
the 'preservation of life'
you: self-righteous rapists
exploiters
and murderers
accuse me of
your crimes!
this is my body

my temple
my domain.

you: mothers   sisters and daughters
who virtuously agree
to give up your bodies to
church and state

beware the sons you birth!
where will you turn
when they bring **you**
to trial?

this is **my** body
to have and to hold
to do with
as i will.

the two worlds of the red nations

'For those who live / in the two worlds: /
There are so few of us, let us / be good /
to one another.'

(from *Southline* by gogisgi / carroll arnett)

-there's no such thing as indians
in north america-
that professor sd to me.
-not like they were, they're
all gone, you know.

(sun dance pole / sweat house pit
four corners marked and colored true
above, below and middle place
corn mother dances green today)

i paused to think what he might mean
and he continued on:
-panama has **real** ones, still **wild**
and **primitive**, not contaminated yet.

(white deer dance / bear dance / eagle dance songs
whale blow / raven step and seal feast
wind spirit whistles / koshare clowns)

-i've spent three summers there   (he sd
-to study them. they're pure.
up here, well, they're americans
like the rest of us. no pure
culture to be found.

(morning star and mountain ways / stomp dance
circle dance / northern and southern styles-clock
and counter clock / up river salmon ceremony / root
digging songs / yei be che huuhuuhuu / shalako blessing)

-they dress and drive and eat fast food, the same
as us. oh-there's remnant bits of this and that,
a few folks speak their native tongue

(blue jeans / cowboy shirts / ten gallon hats
fry bread / navajo tacos / corn-venison-mutton stew
lambing-sheep camp-shearing time / cowboy boots)

-but all in all that's not enough to say
there's any indian culture left
in north america   (he sd

(basket / rainbow / corn and butterfly maidens
acorn mash and corn meal grinding songs
strawberry festival and ribbon shirts / piñon harvest)

five centuries fall away unnoticed
spring plant to harvest to hunt to
silent winter sleep.

long-time stories still live around here
sweet sage, tobacco, cedar and corn pollen
still offered around here.
old time spirit talk and medicine songs
still sung around here.

five centuries now, we walked in two worlds
weaving new stories into baskets and blankets
adding ribbons, beads and bright colored threads
to things we use and wear. work copper, gold
silver, nickel and brass in indian fashion.

five centuries living and dying unnoticed.
five centuries walking silent and hidden.
five centuries in-between 'the two worlds.'

coral woman's song

she looked just like her
daughter-in-law
and i wondered who they were
some other time
while he mixed alarm clocks
and freeways for
revolutions in the mind.

this isn't concrete
(they sd
but nothing follows
when you refuse to agree.

the idea of concreteness
is as illusive as the
obsession that demands
its existence.

circle dancers
among the wi ots
once stomped the earth
back into place
because it tilted
away from the sun.

i circle danced
with a mediterranean tribe
in stockton-
stomping that moment
into place to
coincide with: twenty years
of memories dispersed and
scattered
(returned to dust
coated with asphalt
linked with clocks
and free ways
documented in
my abstract mind.
and they presume
to tell me

—i— must build my **free**ways
with perceivable stuff
limited to their range
of perception

and —i— say:
catch me if you can.

squash blossoms

we chase dawn into sleep
alter days to fit within tendrils of smoke
those fragile trails from dying embers.
what fuel is left to encourage
one last spark into flame?

parchment curls in smoke filled rooms
behind velvet draperies pulled shut.
what spark is left to rekindle
and birth once more?

you spoke of the wolf—lean and close
who knew hunger inside his ribbed coat alone.
i watched greyed countenances wince with recall,
not able to forget firelight fantasies
returning dreams to ashes mixed in sand.

i hear you
out of yesteryears
run back to those places called: used to be.
another time.
another place.

cold despair in soft cushions of dark thought
walks the night through honky tonk bars
stalks neon glow into oblivion
spills lives into various gutters along the way.
the stench of desolation numbs the senses of
the most hardened street cleaners.

fog drifts descend warm and wet
to moisten evening winter streets.

blow the winds of hurricanes
through the eye of the universe
when you exhale living breath.
the alchemists sought only
special material
the sacred fabric of cells transmuted.

the dream is still there
enclosed in fact and fiction
and i feel it surge
through your fingertips
when your hands cup my breasts
and the spark rushes down to
ignite the embers between my thighs
into flames.

notes from san francisco
(1973–1980)

i walk blinded and a new skyscraper
blossoms walls of glass as i pass.
no fog drifts near to obscure my view
or spread mist on my face and hair

late summer hangs heavy with heat.

i hear corn stalks rustle dying leaves
above new winter grass. no strong
laser bridges appear to connect my
sight and mind as my eyes wait for
winter to come.

snow winds hide somewhere else this year.

my fortune rests in diamonds unpurchased
and gold not worn or kept in vaults but
when rubies grow from my fingertips
i will ignite myself and become a star.

tomorrow's history

numbered faces swim
before me
shuffle back and forth
fade into one another
become nerve endings
strung across my
backbone
sink into my shoulder
muscles
cling to me
cry out nightmares as
mute eyes reach out
swim in tears of loss
plead for one heart
to hear words they
cannot speak
feel thoughts they
cannot share and
love they cannot
give
those faces
those eyes reach for
someone to remember
who they might
have been.

dogma of anywhere

1.
precisely at sometime
on a street corner
anywhere
the following events
might take place:

a blind man will walk by and point
a deaf man will say hello
a mute will hurl a word at the sun
and a child will smile
laugh and then wonder
about everything in
anywhere.

40 days of kings and queens
crosses melt in burning sand
cactus sprouts relinquish thorns
relieve the thirsty with their fruit
so carefully grown in arid lands.
a fast will bring visions
and a rich kid who once
walked the desert night
will be born and wish
to be born again.

2.
a shadow slides across a clock.
at the back of a head
dove wings flutter
insist they must remember
the symbols they stand for.

we cry out to all who
approach us to hurry and
catch up to the clock.
it runs faster than it used to
yesterday. speed of thought

is the measure of the
distance we will travel.

turn around if you would
meet your future arriving at its
precisely appointed moment.

turn around and meet yourself
once again and you will
find you are in another time

just equidistant from right now
in anywhere.

dialogue : subjunctive mode

from each race: unique

we come to attempt to
dialogue. a difficult thing
this coming together to
gather ideals buried ahead of us.

what we talk now
has been done—but
we remembered our future's
present! and changed the
words to fit **this** now.

>   he sd)
>   chomsky's profound structure
>   was a commonality to all people's.
>   we were rigged that way—
>   prior to learning.
>
>   i sd)
>   you cannot talk wrong!
>
>   it is an act that requires
>   conscious consideration-
>   the formulation of idea constructs
>   follows neuronal patterns
>   fired in serial fashion—
>
>   therefore: the progression of
>   all language proceeds in
>   a one-way direction.

it is a difficult thing—this coming together.
we do not comprehend our children—
these youths who propose to destroy

hard won ideals
profound structures and
old ways of seeing who
we have become

but this process
we come to particularize
has become: the describer set:

the limit guide
of the **doing** of the **then**
those pastperfect actions
<u>toward</u>——this place.

the song: the dance :   the poem
                        (for charles olson

1.
i toil   in the field
syllable into line
through the breath.
the breathing is
difficult
the birthing.

i dreamed of you   mama,
far away,   talking hours
into the night.
the breathing was difficult
and you changed again
trying to tell me something
i couldn't remember   -except
the field was there and
stretched on and on.

the stubble would not
be replaced with new corn
and spring is soon.

the breathing is
difficult at times
from syllable into line.

the song :   the dance :   the poem
                        (for robert creeley

2.
i am sent to the fields
to labor once more.
the breathing will not
discover the line.
my land races visions
before my eyes
tunes these senses i possess

to smell and taste and touch
yet   -the solidity of a
sandstone boulder
will not be painted without a brush.

        my pen is frozen
        in some ancient mold
        in tubes of paint.
the image lost   wants only to hide
in my palette's colors
        -will not be found
        to mould a line.

what syllable then can best convey
the ochre/umbers of that ground?
and choking dust that's interlaced
        with sunburst prism
        on window glass?

i swell with visions
erupting rocks and clouds
within my mind.
i know this wilderness in my blood
and cannot sing it
into line.

the song : the dance : the poem
              (for robert duncan

3.
as climate reaches roots
together with polar infinities
moss springs from the cracks
in the line
grasps energy seeded in context
replaced as a function
for internal rhyme.

these roots go back somewhere.
related through syllable

through time
connect with a script not known.
some form that communicated
alternative meanings
still held in this construct
in this now.

that master who began to
define this form
remarked upon the search:
the detective part of the work
any creation comes from.

the **doing** will suffice.
the momentum of the forward push
the breath : defines the line.

life is the breathing / life breath
embues each syllable chosen
energized-
embodied within the creation
jam / packed into content.
that moss will recede - that remark
made to remember the roots.

trace roots from branches
branches from leaves
each word floats   -caught
suspended in time
reveals energy connected ancestors
as each syllable selected moves
more living breath through
the line.

wolf stories

1.
the changing of the guard becomes
final every day.
reinforcements show us the places
of the average.

that the captain of the guard appears as often as
any two-gun hero goes frequently unnoticed.
                    it's the common touch
                    i'm looking for (despite
                    the fact that bizarre is
                    what i often find.

an age of miracles proclaimed ordinary with:
a certain amount of nostalgia for the past (he sd

                    i wanted to make note of what he sd
                    it was a good line and i had begun to
                    weave an intricate image in my head
                    while the conversation continued.
                    i cannot breathe today, but remember
                    other days of going everywhere
                    world round   -and revolutionary.

the romantic and the pretty are kind of phony
even seedy elegance isn't straight   (he sd

his symbols surround a momentary breath.
whatever did he mean by disclosing his
traumatic childhood to the ladies aid society?

slices of lives
alien pictures caught in handholds
we call time our desperation
and wonder at a different
set of choices.

2.
mooncars
covered with dust and polished ores
a millenium in evolution

rock gently in warehouse night lights.
ergs and dynes of wasted energy
dispossess me of positive emotion
reverse the process back through me
and release a negative imprint.

mind trestles waver.
a muddy mire reaches out
to grasp my foot
pulls me down from jagged rocks
paincoated with learning
how to move in time
-alone.

this motion is wasted   (she sd
light is a negative filled
with solid objects   is
the positive foreground
we pretend we perceive
and could not   without it.

i cannot move the levers of
my mind to alter anything
but i can hear a knell
canted from the vast darkness
inhabited by stars.

3.
selective bargaining stills the
most perceptive intuition.

the hanging trees bend
with the wait   of bodies
no longer visible.

to solicit a point of view
requires a basic agreement
on reference points

like: serpentine from madagascar
and limpet harems   in   the sea.

flint stories

1.
to postpone the ridiculous
is imminently impossible
although all preceding events
disclose the whimsy of the moment:
          the distortion level of which
          must remain an arbitrary choice.

the barest meaning
of innocence is an
incommunicable dilemma
beside the sophisticated
interpretations attached on
all sides.

pointed fingers
compel me to
dodge the blows
i might inflict:
          my boomerangs
          come home to rest.

2.
the puzzle implied complexity
                    yet
described simplicity of game.

each piece moved counter to
                    the clock
intent on such liberal display as
seemed necessary to hide behind.
the clockwise movement
                    of an indeed wise clock
                    went unnoticed
by the players at the board.

the talleys counted conservatives
to be more prominent than not
and diehard radicals entirely missing

from the scheduled events
                    (although black and white hats
equalized at the prescribed point on the scale.

note that puzzled players result from
countering any game's natural flow.
                    clockwise movers
                    resolve the puzzle with
timely attention and resolution.

(to solve the puzzle:
                    move wisely.

3.
the face of a benevolent man
dissolves into diabolical crimsons.
his jolly laugh and mirth filled eyes
sink deep into sly looks of
whispers crowded with
cunning and stealth-
invites the careless to
partake of froth
and fireworks.

chartreuse deepening greens
flood into violets
forge shape and line to
disclose the coming events
of a disneyland show.

no cellophane or stretch & seal
can keep out the colorful noise.
sirens build tension
choke halls with smoke screens
and faked displays of
what could be but won't (he sd

                              (we sd
it was all so useless -anyway.

4.
hurry!   hurry!   hurry!

fasten your seatbelts—adjust your goggles
and be prepared to submerge.
the descent is long   -but quick
unless you resist the gravitational pull.
resistance will cause a shock that can
short circuit an entire network-
fusing all recorded imagery into
overlapping fuzzy renditions of what was.
the vortex of the whirlpool
is relatively calm.   deadly quiet.
                    (as in the eye of a hurricane.
in between the edge and the eye
the holocaust abides
                    (to bend and shape
                    or break the whole
to scatter the bits into anonymity
into never was.

no mark: no place:
no name: no face:

the work is going well.
wires hum with intricate communications
                    reaching proper destinations.
impedence levels below tolerance all clear for
the next issue of communiqués.

the speed of thought squared is yesterday-
the day before you wind up back in yourself
                    (she capsuled with capable ease.

5.
straightlaced—filled with
double standards-
the invaders come from
monuments of stone
down the hill into changelings.
come up against untouched feelings
                    and unseen lives

lost in freedom.

the invaders carry
slabs of slate still
marked with symbols to
impose upon all the strange
and different ones they meet.

unable to lift their eyelids
            (bathed in shadow and cologne
they cling to locks- chainlink- barbedwire-clutching their bits of slate
                as keepsake
                as keepsafe.

the invaders still come down
steep hills and mountainsides
into double standard doubletalk changelings-
stand between lives and
images of lives-
                    separate.

                    isolate.
                    violent.

6.
hang 'em.   don't shoot 'em.
the arc of the swing describes
the whole story. a short one but-
                        it doesn't matter.
the old man who springs the trap
doesn't care too much either.
it's just another job.
                    none of us
could ever figure out why he did it.
                    we tried for awhile
                    then gave up.

the story covered the whole mass of
                    human passions.
the play goes on: tense   -most of the time
even with all action missing
(no violence allowed except in

thought or memory.
missing in action.
repeat. deviate. repeat. radiate.
repeat. change. repeat the pattern.
the whole mass of human passions
missing in action.

shoot 'em.   don't hang 'em.
it's quicker
if not cleaner.

fox tales - 1

finally!
the escape hatch
opened—
a cloud of steam
seven guppies
three sea horses
and a giant squid
floated upward
headed landward
then decided to
stay where they were.

meanwhile:
fifteen supersonic jets
buzzed a single atoll
on their lunch break
shaking loose:

nine coconuts
to rattle their way
along the beach
to stop
a hundred and
fifty yards from:
seven guppies
three sea horses
a giant squid
a cloud of steam.

(and fox smiled.

fox tales - 2

but–
i can't.

the fence is
too tall
can't climb
that high-
that way.
chain link
brick tile
barbed wire
all the same
impossible walls
i can't!
you see-
i never
learned
how to
climb.

(and fox winked.

fox tales - 3

inside his head
it's dark.
no light bulb
flashing.
no brilliant forms
to expand
beyond-
outside of
darkened chambers.

cracked: once or twice
to let more dark
inside
crowds out twilight
leaves shadows
to disappear
slowly.

i can't
SEE—!!
(he sd
p-l-e-a-s-e turn off
the guiding
light.

(and fox chuckled.

fox tales - 4

besides the sunglasses
a few bottle tops
and tin cans
the street
walked empty
holding up its privacy
for bargain-
a bright red juicy
apple or the ripest
plum in the box.
it offered anonymity
with its purchase
allowing the buyer
to discard
unwanted bits of self
within it.

the sunglasses
belonged to the
previous owner.

(and fox went away.

old medicine stories

san francisco - collingwood street

in my dream: an albino crow—and
children carrying coffins behind their eyes
starched stiff and straight: marching.
to simplify complexity was the herculean task i chose.

the lyric and the metaphor simply done was how
she phrased it—and you must search for words
to act as holograms (she sd
do not force the word into the **object**
or confuse the **object** with its name.
these limitations **stop** the world and forget
the chance that—changing offers (she sd
was it choices then, i dreamed about?
or some meaningful configuration of
        a symbol clue?
        a language stop?
        a feeling tone?
        a metaphor?

any mind sieved for easy filtering refuses to
contain this evidence for further reckoning—
for what pyramid or monument was lately
built to last ten thousand sun turns
that would not erode the shape of its
original conception?

i sd) counting roomsful of barley
and millet seed was just as easy
as dreaming holograms of crows
and marching pyramids
under ancient suns.

(1978)

san francisco - collingwood street

the power drum was near the center
the choosing of it carefully done
some configuration placed precisely end on end
stacked in proper fashion, to season just right
was what (she sd
(i heard her in my sleep

a special wood for making drums—
it seems important you should
know how it is done (she sd
you must sketch a line, a forty-five degree angle
you see; you must stack the wood in lines
not up and down but leaning out — just so
for the proper seasoning:
   these drums will be for dances
   these will be for hunts
   these for ceremonials

the drums used for healing only will be buried in
the driest ground underneath the rest
a fire will then be built on top
just large enough to warm the earth above
where they will rest until the healers
come to claim them.

hunters will come for the animal drums
singers will come for the dancing drums
seers will come for the ceremonial drums
all the rest will be destroyed.
chopped apart. scattered
to the sacred directions.

and that's how it's to be done (she sd
that's how it's done.

(1978)

". . .wouldn't it be strange if this
is how our life turned out?. . ."
-from *The Deer Hunter*

san francisco - 10th avenue

never stretches out to enclose a
careless thought shed at someone's feet.
we walk an unknown future pictured
once and now forgotten in today's tensions.

battlefields emerge around us
spread burning bodies to be looked at
examined closely for: just cause.

disparate ideas flung helter-skelter
by unnamed marksmen leave charred minds
on display as evidence of their handiwork
while yet another forum for dialogue
hides beneath media barrages of:
how life should be lived.
we sit. entranced. vacant bodies left as
testimonial to these assorted jobs —well done.

assaulted souls remember ghost dance circles
reclaim those painted ceremonial shirts
rush to embrace any savior bold enough to
offer up their being for: decimation.

centuries interlock. the line of demarcation
blurred by volcanic ash   —the fourth world
rumbles its prophetic endings
as we remain unmoved   unshakeable in
our tract houses in: steel town coaltown
lumbertown wheattown corntown cottontown

unconcerned in our musings.

(1979)

san francisco - 10th avenue

the displacement was vague.
cantilevered. lopsided. omnidirectional.
all applied. nighttime and fog shrouds
begin to drape multileveled structures-
caress them into obscurity

the curve of space demands a line from nowhere.
bounced back on itself —will include all
invisible frequencies.
science and social dogma can plot these
invisible realities for our physical beings.
we claim faith as our form of understanding.

industry specializes in transmuting the curves of
graphs into knowable touchable events; always
successful —they. societies of shamans (medicinemen
medicinewomen) consistently fail to disclose the
properties of our success —yet tabulate our
failures quite well.

the bessemer process launched the tooling
of a new world while unrelated bits of psyche
strained and filtered through the freud process
exploded into alienation —revolution and counter
mechanisms of every invisible shape and kind.

the fog grows larger —claiming more particles from
invisible processes unknown bombings wars ending revolutions
beginning—becomes substance
contaminates all it touches
        and
we make sacrifice
to the encompassing grey gloom
assume loss of all sunlight in our
generation of foreseeable time.

(1979)

174

santa fe new mexico

a pearl handled revolver
with one silver bullet
hides in my mind—
      the savages are loose
      around these parts
      a small voice whispers
      in the crowd—
a young masked man strode into the bar
strode out on the street strode into the shops
      i'm the lone ranger
      (he exclaimed to a broad
      variety of hidden smiles
      and averted eyes.

haciendas climb these hillsides
huddle in old river beds
people and houses walled in walled out
there are walls everywhere
chain link adobe red brick cinder block
      ¿y quien queres a ver?
      ¿y quien quieres a entrar?

welcome to the big city of santa fe (he sd
as the cloud people gathered to make sparks
put on one hellava light show to invite
the rain gods to visit the fields.
      it's not the distance that counts
      but the approach that matters
      (somebody sd

she sd) go away cloud people —no rain today
come back some other time
maybe those fences will be down
then you can walk through all the fields
kissing cornchildren into growth.
making movies and art in this exotic town
      call new moments into being
      silver bullets and rusty nails-
      green chili and beans and corn
      tortillas will feed us while we wait.

gentlemen (she sd
you'll find your minds in the bottom drawer-

(1980)

reno nevada

she watched loner
catwalking through a gambling den
dealing himself a losing hand

you pretty, fella (she sd
got the lean look low down
gaitor gait
you something else you
know what i mean?
flicked her eyes
across his soul
moved on down the street.

oh the tears lie buried and the shadows call
as the night barks cold in the neon sights
and the long grass hides from this winter sun
as the pale ones move through the land.
                    the long bones
                    the hollow bones
                    the dry bones rattle.

the jazz lady sings light funky blues
many times, many times and from the
other side of the world comes
the blue-eyed voice of the quiet man
through birch and pine on a lengthy wind.
it's my kind of music (he sd
smashing! passionate! romantic! music!
makes you want to fall in love
each time you hear it!   and you-
you are blessed (he sd —you are well
you are rich with exotic history!

oh the years lie buried and the shadows fall
on the wrinkled fold in the morning light

176

the vanishing point hides the buffalo track
as the pale ones move through the land.
        the long bones
        the hollow bones
        the dry bones rattle
        beneath this desert sand.

nickel/clink — quarter/clak — dollar/clunk
buzzer bells mark payoffs pays the taxes
place your bets drop your coins pull the handles

    brother eagle brother hawk
    circle round
    know many things
watch the people in conestoga wagons
appear/disappear/reappear
watch the people in buses trains cars and planes
appear/disappear/reappear
melt into mazes of light

    brother eagle brother hawk
    circle round
    know many things.

oh the tears lie buried and the shadows call
as the night barks cold in the neon sights
the long grass hides from this winter sun
as the pale ones move through the land.
        the long bones
        the hollow bones
        the dry bones rattle
            many times
            many times
            many times
            many times.

(1980)

journeys i, ii, iii

journeys i

san francisco - march 1987
1.
to become a mendicant
i lift my bones
onto the path and
enter into myself

pride precludes
my holding a begging
bowl in outstretched hand
(my eyes downcast

unable to process gold
into useable notions or
ideologies. this late lesson
transforms other meanings

other lives into new fruits
to nourish my spirit.
i take sustenance from
chance encounters

unravel moments and
time junctions to examine
lives and places once
tenanted by me.

san francisco - march 1987
2.
that she
who digs roots   (from some
ancient past
kneels beneath her memory

of a future 'with pyramid'
this sudden insight of
my painted vision
provokes congruent memories

in me. a self portrait (you sd
had i considered the possibility?
no conscious or imagined application
was my reply.

yet - this small peninsula
bounded by salt and bay waters
has been peaceful home to me
to us; this once sacred ground

to ancient souls who hunted
and rested here.
root digger. basket weaver.
tule grass collector. remembered.

münchen - april 1987
3.
in münchen, i walked
warmly dressed against
strong cold winds through
gardens once known to me

I soaked up sunlit snow
and people playing ice
games on frozen canals.
now a city park, i remember

when this broad avenue
heard münchener nobles laugh
and shout preparing for afternoons
of indoor swimming, hunting parties

or picnics among these dense groves.
today this castle and its small lodges
are grand museums that still
hold untold stories from other days.

maybe the grounds keepers and
curious tourists imagine what
royal life was like when kings and
queens lived here. i stare through

windows and wonder if the songs
sighs, laughter and tears of my other
self are still caught in the thick silence
that clings to the sculptured ceilings

and high walls of schloss nymphenburg.
this familiar place
this castle,
these grounds
my castle town.

for franz marc
(kunsthalle - münchen
4.
you dreamed blue horses
in fields and mazes of color
painted your visions with
bold tones and strong lines

landschaften and so much light
spill from your canvases
ride waves of emotion
through my heart and drench

my cheeks with recognition
of you. 1914: and the power
of your thoughts explode
through your brush—

if i look close enough
at "two forms fighting"
i might find your goodbye note:
that certain point

of poised flight from your
confinement in rectangles
(of every kind   and your
reach for universal spirit.

saarbrücken - april 1987
5.
saarland belches
smoke and steam through
metal pipes
directly into heaven
while spewing steel ingots
into the outstretched hands
of deutsche customers.

once a land of bitter struggles ·
for coal driven industries
peopled now with
bilingual nationals its
border towns confuse
ausländer (saarlouis in
deutschland and wildeweiss in
frankreich. at the edge of the
ancient maginot line, a new
industrial giant commands
obeisance of the alsace-lorraine.

here—across the border
from saarbrücken
four fat steel and concrete
towers drive impressive
clouds of steam into the
arms of an unsuspecting future.
historians may one day note
this small town set cozily
on the west bank of the mosell
known in this time as:
catenom.

journeys ii

> . . .you have a long way to go.
> walk carefully, speak politely
>
> to those who have done their worm-cycle,
> for gods have been smashed before
>
> and idols and their secret is stored
> in man's very speech,
>
> in the trivial or
> the real dream. . .
>
> (from "The Walls Do Not Fall"
> by h. d.

münchen - april 1987
1.
what secrets then, do we store today
in our dreams?
in our mundane daily acts?
in our 'very speech'?

which precious moment
carries more value?
the one preceding?
the one following?

which dull event lies
waiting to become a
momentous awakening or
even greater catastrophe
in the mind of the receiver?

maria switzerland - 1987
2.
in dreams.
caricatures people the
events of my days:
discourse about grotesque
trivialities; spoken sentences
skewed to correspond with
images too absurd to frighten me.
i quickly record this
surreal landscape before dawn
wanting only to release
those disfigured forms of
mistaken identities into a
different atmosphere.

3.
i am overcrowded
with waiting to get away
from being filled with
duffel bags; 'not all my
stuff' (i sd
but we put it into a dented
yellow truck and trailer
anyway. 'there's no more
room' (i sd
no room for me
to fit in front or
in back and the mystery
unravels and shapeshifts
into vapor trails
across the evening skies.

4.
i moved your left eye aside
to see out: there was no
room for me in you.
i was gorged
with so much "stuff,"

your left cheek split open
my love - trying to
make room for me;
trying to hold me
filled with too many
incidents and meaningless
aspirations.
i moaned to see your broken face
and closed your eye to
heal the bloodless wound.

5.
how patient we are
to discover our symbols
whispered secrets
shared lifetimes.

how clever to remember
landscapes, altitudes
atmospheric pressures.

i found your treasure
accidentally- running
through days of rainbow
visions i wanted to catch
and plant for our future.
if i had not stumbled, i
would not have noticed you
waiting for me,
splitting open for me.

you came to the
back door of my dreams
and rescued me
in your yellow truck.

münchen - 1987
6.
ritual cleansing
enlightened with knowledge
candles and heat lamps
provides my patient cells
loving acceptance.

in concert
they blend into
harmonious community life
preparing the whole 'us'
for new journeys into
unremembered days to come.

fatigue reflected in overcast skies
flows out with shifting thoughts;
points of reference on the
celestial map of human endeavor.

i call myself into being again
and this now awakens
connected layers and
levels of mysteries forever
held in gentle times.

(hexen nacht in münchen at the negerhalle)
7.
they gathered to dance themselves
into remembrance of "the old ways"
black leather tough replaced
the white gauze that clung
gracefully to the women
once tending the temples of
venus, isis and astarte.

the steel tower in the negerhalle
left by the war god they
came to destroy-
invaded their space with
his ghostly presence and
the name of this momentary
'temple' - matched their dress
and their inclinations.

journeys iii

munich - 5/5/87
1.
you ask me who i am
and don't notice who you are

call up yourself, your powerful spirit
practice this moment once again

i hold the rainbow in my teeth
spin dew filled webs with strands of hair

sing flowers into bloom
cry snowstorms in my sleep

i am the sun, the wind
the rain, the stars.

you ask me who i am
and forget we are the same

i carry clouds to hide behind
make fog to cover you

breathe fire into baking ovens
plant my thoughts in budding nebulae

you ask me who i am
forget woman is my name

i am earth and sky
and universe

and i know you are
the same.

munich - 5/8/87
2.
clouds move sideways
reveal stars above
a gothic spire

we call them out of darkness
to tell ourselves once more:
wherever we cast our true selves
we are discovered.
later we journey into
forests of illusions
unable to find our way back
to the image of a cloudless sky.

he should help her (you sd
i mentioned something about
meddling with natural
design and (you sd
other male birds help
female birds, why can't
this one have that too?

in my mind i traced
coal into diamonds instead
of rubies - turquoise
nesting in quartz and
copper salts instead of iron oxide
just then i stumbled into clay
my thoughts
mud-thick and culpable.
i dodged the mirror but saw
myself staring back, a ray of
recognition distorting my image
aha - i am meddling too (i sd
and watched mica schist
spring garnets blood red
in memory.

munich - 5/11/87

3

think only of wonder and sunshine-
shadows cannot grow in brilliant light

sing lullabyes and
laugh walls away from:
        around your heart
        around your eyes
        around your town

walk bridges into unknown places
smile the people you meet
into being.
        cry for love lost
        cry for love gained

hold hands with old people who
look at your life and remember
themselves
notice the child who will
replace you and won't recall
your name.

look at yourself in mirrors
as often as you can-
be glad you are   live
hold life in your hands
place it in all you touch
love yourself each day
you are here and
the world will be glad
you were born.

neuschwanstein - 5/17/87
(for ludwig II
4.
pöllat gorge echoes the footsteps
of a haunted young king
across the slender maríenbrücke—
clouds cling together collecting
river mist and release it at sunset
as i examine this never completed
monument with wonder.

ludwig—your guilded königschlösser carry
memories and carefully crafted ideals
embedded in hidden technology and
unfinished dreams.
so intent were you on leaving
the exquisite arts and crafts of
your times to a more knowledgeable
future—you drove your artisans to
produce their very best works
and the treasury you emptied has
been refilled by countless visitors to
'mad ludwig's' castles. sad ludwig:
bathed in swans and alpine snows
lost in bavarian forests and inland seas.

rejected visions and visionaries
hold banquets among ordinary thoughts—
this future i inhabit
recognizes your ageless vision
and determination.
i reach into the space around me
to find the moments you spent
with carver and carpenter, painter
and joiner, architect and musician

i see you pace the walks
of herrenchiemsee;
know you are sailing
in the gondola of
venus grotto;
that you sit at
your desk in linderhof;

while
the winds still sigh your name
in pöllat gorge.

munich - 5/30/87
5.
ich habe zwei leben
two lives in two different worlds
yet simultaneous:
wienerschnitzel und weissbier
für abendessen in münchen
freue ich mich.

i straddle the atlantic ocean
and shift directions in my mind
der westliche ozean von hier
und wo die sonne untergeht aber
where the sun rises i
greet morning in california.

zwei leben habe ich
combined in memory
gothic or baroque cathedrals
und kirchen
adobe churches pacific west winds
and foggy summer beaches.

bavarian spring in the allgäu
blooms early fields with schneeglöckchen
to replace winter bettdecke
then shifts to yellow flowers creating
new carpets of schlüsselblumen
stitched into bright green
backgrounds everywhere.

riegsee ammersee plansee und starnbergersee
move from whites to greys to rich blue greens
and the buchen und birken bäume
clothe their dark skeletons
color the spaces in alpine forests
with new leaves

notes from central california

1. transitions & reflections

hollow echoes bounce off
morning freight trains
heading north
heading south.   their
crossing whistles
mourn country tunes
          (midnite blues harps
and this moment suspended in
my thoughts.
another day passing, counted-
i am not involved in more than
moving pen across paper
to record some half forgotten
memory; some other place in mind
where i dedicated myself
to an heroic ideal.

what strange force drove me
so far from the sleepy
new mexico town
of my childhood; from
the ordinary accomplishments of
warm hearth, warm home;
from the pride of
good wife, good mother ?

my babies grew too quickly
for us to notice we survived
the crossing-
how we held onto dreams
larger than our
combined understanding
could grasp.

i am here in central california
          (another sleepy town
in quiet isolation;
have left all i built
behind me
once again.

i could have failed so grandly
beside days of
dropping out-
rebellious and intent
on revolution,

but i am caught in motion
toward concrete
slowed just long enough to
notice i can't change
the cycle of the moon
the echo of a whistling freight train
the arbitrary definition of
any state of being.

-we should be thankful
we don't get shot
for being poets in america (she sd
        (but ignored poems can kill the
        spirit of revolutionary intent
        much like bullets kill bodies
        (i sd

2. gardens & killing fields

most days, i only notice the
textures of affluence
all around me;
warm days and cool nights-
the joy of being close to
plants and critters in my garden.
california in continuous blossom.
late fall and early winter where
tulips, hyacinths
and daffodils insist on breaking through.
the iris are in bloom again
and the hollyhocks
and the roses.
i love my garden in november
in central california
and i'm content
most days.

yesterday, i quit 'passing' here
as a colorless neutral— and
spoke harshly of omissions
in our poetic conversations.
the responses
ground harshly into my brain
attached themselves to other phrases
handed back to me
across the years—
over and over.
        (she's not color
        but she was poor white—
        working class—entitled
        to fame **and** outrageous
        speaker's fees. . .
right on mama, right on.

some days, i wake to the sounds
of a mother's moaning—still
sobbing softly 'cause the baby
just died. not in ethiopia—
but in east oakland.
some days,
a black mother's bitter cry
pierces my morning reverie 'cause
they brought her teen-age boy
back home to her filled
with heroin and bullet holes
in east oakland—
not south africa.

some days invade my
sense of well being
in tidy central california—
and i can't make the sobbing stop.
that american indian mother
who found a syringe
in her son's jacket pocket
along with a handful of
'reds' and 'yellows', cries out
in east oakland.
i hear them in the middle of
uplifting discourse about

language and literature;
       (hear those cambodian mothers
       those laotian mothers
       those thai mothers
       those mexican, nicaraguan,
       salvadorean, guatemalan mothers
in east oakland
in east oakland.

i watch unreal moments
on late night tv
sponsored by christian charities
well meaning movie stars or rock stars
but i can't seem to find
benefits for dying children
in east oakland or
in east l.a.

no big name poets
organizing marathon readings—
no political rallies or demonstrations
to stop drug traffic to children
in east oakland
in east st. louis
in east l.a.

familiar phrases are waiting
to leap on me
i know them—
i heard them at the rally to support allende
when i asked about the mothers in
the san francisco 'mission' with hungry children
who couldn't speak english, were too proud
or too afraid to ask a gringo for help—
and he sd)
-that's a domestic issue, man-
we've got to stop the c.i.a.!

at the rally to support cuba
she sd)
-they've got clinics and welfare—
job core, title 4 & 6 & 20

in the barrio. my people are
starving in cuba and chile.

at the rally to save the whales
i sd)
-my people are starving in
south dakota and dying at pit river
and pine ridge
and he sd)
-that's a domestic issue. whales
are an endangered species globally
we've got to stop this senseless
killing. . .
            (in the pacific and atlantic oceans
not in gallup, tuba city, east l.a., harlem, south bronx
clear lake, tucson, san antonio, pit river, detroit
not in wounded knee, south dakota
not in east oakland, california.

oh—i know the phrases
waiting behind the eyes
of the saviors of the trees
dogs, cats, ranch minks
coyotes, bobcats, condors, falcons and
alligators. i read the flyers
and solicitations for donations
and wonder at the paper costs
the printing costs
the mailing costs—

oh—i admire the concern
the care, the organizations
the volunteers, the crack-down
on drunk drivers and don't begrudge
the dollars that pour into ethiopia or
mexico, or colombia; that pour into
organizing demonstrations against
south africa against nuclear weapons
against toxic waste and pollution
it's all relevant, all related.

my pen moves with difficulty
tolling contradictions

knowing i'll soon be 'busted'
and fined for not wearing
a seat belt when i drive or
smoking in an airplane or public
building; knowing those fines will
disappear into higher salaries
new highways, new sewer and
water systems while children
continue to die
in the killing fields
of our own backyards.

oh no — i don't have the courage
to walk alone in east oakland or
attract a pusher's bullet
in east l.a.—
i live in tidy central california
and most days, i'm content.

but today i heard the sobbing again
tasted the silent terror
and desperation of all those mothers
with my morning coffee
as i flipped the tv dial
and scanned the local papers
for the announcements about
the star-studded benefit concert
for the children in the **killing fields**
all over america.
i was searching for
the thousands of demonstrators
marching to save our children
from drug pushers
in east st. louis
in east l.a.
in east oakland—

oh—i know it's a domestic issue
and they've got programs, cops and
concerned citizens handling domestic issues
oh yes—**this senseless killing**
has got to **s t o p** right now
        'cause mothers are still cryin

      and babies are still dyin
      and children are comin home
      full of heroin and bullet holes
in east st. louis
in east l.a.
in east oakland
in east oakland
in east oakland

san luis obispo/santa margarita/santa barbara

1. how tall our heroes were

we missed the parade that night,
where **was** the car-ni-vál?

we caught a glimpse of
glitter on the street dis/solving
into pubs and eateries-
a party crowd on
mardi gras eve
shouting at each other

while the tv in the corner
snatched lulls in conversation
trying to entertain us with
the newest video rock tune

but we entertained ourselves-
roared laughter at each
other over loud voices around us
and saturday night video tunes.
was this carnival? mardi gras?
                    -why not? (i sd

(no substance here—no
careful thought
no layered meaning yet inscribed
upon this storytelling page-

we drank beer and spoke of
things and places been
noted points of variance-
discussed our backgrounds
our beginnings and
the lack of substance in
contemporary literature;

discussed
historical heroes and
fictional lake communities

and the almost fictional
chumash natives of this
central california coast.

                        (then i sd
-embedded substance
like buried nuggets
demands mental detectors
skillfully operated by
prospectors for meaning.

elemental ores in various
combinations wait to be
unearthed, leached and separated
into different vats;
weighed, sifted, filtered
then recombined again
and again until all the
relationships are noticed
until all the stories have been told.

some of our historical and literary
heroes **were** tall
and far bolder
more innovative than we
future generations
may find treasure buried
in our mundane writings;
and this central coast
will one day yield more than
the bones of those unknown,
unnamed native chumash heroes
that preceeded us.

some of our heroes are unknown to us

the fathers/los padres surround us;
hold free life and no tresspass
behind the same fence
while los osos/the bears stand watch

between the fathers and
el mar pacifico/the peaceful water.

somewhere
in this region, ancient rocks
carry picture stories about
a happening that seemed
important to make note of.

the exact meanings
are lost to me.
the translators were
re/educated and baptized
into new beginnings.

'running bear' became 'josé'
'little deer' turned into 'ignacio'
'bird with no song' was called 'esperanza'
and 'quiet water' married a 'lopez'
who left **his** name as the
origin of that laguna/lake
outside arroyo grande/the big dry wash.

my pen cracks ink
into the blanks;
ignores recent historical
coatings of asphalt conquests
and old victorians oozing with
substance and legend.

ignores yet older missions
(those pearls of civilization
whipped from blood caked mud
by fra junipero serra-
testaments to the victory of
bartolomé de las casas:
champion of the heathen souls.

renamed, replaced
civilized into encomiendas
re/invented on the spot.
san—santa

san—santa
san—santa

"ruega por nosotros
nuestro padre, nuestro señor."
(pray for us
our father, our lord)

santa barbara, san ardo
san juan bautista, santa maria
santa rosa, san miguél
san ysidro, santa ynéz
renamed, replaced
re-invented on the spot.

in 1548
great scholars, great thinkers
journeyed to valladolid—
royal capital of carlos cinco
el rey of 16th century spain
to debate the true nature
of those native inhabitants
of nueva españa.

juan ginés sepulveda,
world renowned scholar and jurist
called them slaves!
natural slaves as described in
aristotelian doctrine (that great
ancestor of american thought
and argued for a papal bull-
a declaration to the world
of the soulless nature of los índios
inhabiting the new world.

but—the dominican padre,
insisted the indian contained
a soul!
could be civilized
should be baptized
and saved!

for three years they battled
at the court of carlos cinco
and in 1550
holy mother church and
bartolomé de las casas
won the day,
the soul of the indian,
and moral sanction
to proceed with conquest
in the name of diós
and carlos rey of spain.

san—santa
san—santa
san—santa
san luis obispo
san juan capistrano
santa margarita
san ramón.

somewhere around here,
ancient rocks carry
picture stories about
pre/balboan times
of heroic moments
and ordinary days
that missionized 'juanita'
might interpret for me

or maybe old man 'pedro's'
grandfather, chumash 'diego,'
remembers the stories
his grandfather
told about coyote
the tides
the whales
the mollusks
the swallows
grasses and grains
sun - moon - and earth
and the nine thousand year history
of the chumash people.

mardi gras 1986 recounted
documented,
retold.
mr. lincoln
was a tall man   (we sd
a hero and a paradox
                    (we sd

bartolomé de las casas
was a hero
and a paradox
and — some of our heroes
are still unknown
to us

renamed, replaced
re-invented on the spot.

from she) poems

she) moved forward because
she) could no longer
hold the surfaces together
around her
they continually raised dust
would not glow anymore
no matter what
she) did or   (sd
and the yellow / grey
reflected everywhere
inside and out

she) pondered unyielding concepts
become daily presents to
unwrap quickly then
stow away on closet shelves
and reexamine on
another day.

she) wanted to remain a spy
undisturbed in her passivity
or a confirmed marxist with
no new creed to expound

the crisp edge of this
hallucination cut through his
tongue-thick-wobbly-words—
she) told herself the difference
was doing or not doing
the stuff they called
their life.

#####

she) inhabited her universe tenaciously
holding onto the crevices and tiny
bits of obsidian singlemindedly-
her days froze in unison
and sometimes slid past each other
with no marks or scratches
for identification

occasionally
her memory coincided with a
particular day and
a forgotten friend
came to call

the visits began with gossip to share
out of date events to re-examine
and put away with several
cups of coffee and
halfapack of cigarettes

she) reached conclusions that
heralded a new combination
of possibilities-

the friend always carried a
personal message for her
unaware most of the time
that s/he did so-   but
she) knew
and the messages
she) sent herself
moved her into other dreams.

#####

she) wanted roses once a month
because she deserved them
she) believed that giving
was connected to loving
but she was wrong in
this case

she) wanted to tell him
that everytime he won
he lost more than he
could measure when the
tallies were counted

she) mourned those days of
intense drama

the words they flung
and emotional
roller coasters he and
she) had constantly created—

she) told herself
she) wanted peaceful quiet and
silent loving as replacement
high drama was too hard—
required huge frames of reference
meticulous accounting and
far too much energy to
track down the story plots
they hatched spontaneously—
at random.

she) dreamed simplicity
over and over while
detailed scenes from the
forties and fifties of
uniformed-g.i.-joes—
turned-cowboys
dancing rock & roll
floated about in her
consciousness—

she) added deep longing
for spice—focused her will
to strengthen the wish
and finally
her dream came true.

######

in germany
she) thought about courage
and blood lines
her indian identity
entitlements and the
american dream
the vanishing indian
playing indian

taking dog & pony shows
around the world and
her nonindian identity

she) considered the frenzy
of documentation
in 'indian country'
exploration of detail
examination of culture
and family life
in 'nonindian country'
gave explanations
interpretations of all
symbolical references—
the meaning of this
the reason for that

are you real?
          (they ask
do you still make ceremonies
with dances and song?
          (they ask
or are you just acting without
knowing the meaning ?
          (they want to know

she) heard their questions
outside her surprised thoughts of
          what are they saying? —oh
          they're hunting for indians—
          for real indians!

she) joined in on the projections
and explanations
dredged details from experience
to meet expectations
then lulled herself into compliance
with the scholarly tasks
at hand

she) remained transfixed by
this continued attention

toward every possibility of
indigenous aboriginal life

she) listened to monologues
listened to dialogues
heard all arguments
understood the necessity
for 're-inventing the
enemy's language'
and wondered when this wave
would crash into all the
other waves gone before.

in years past
she) had visited celtic
shrines and ludwig's castles
talked with shamans and
healers from various
parts of the world

she) had danced in
the dali lama's space
moved parallel to
his movements in time—
coalesced energies within
nearby circles
in the mountains and
valleys among the
people who called her there.

#####

she) pursued her versions
of reality
continued to separate
the caustic from
the sublime
reexamined anecdotal
testimonials
and wondered:

why on earth would anyone
want to discover nothingness?
                (she sd

she) stumbled upon an argument
over enlightenment
almost entered the fray
with her usual
            -yes but
            what about—
oh my
she) was guilty—oh yes—of
thought and deed contrary
to mainstream
whimsical fancies—

                -hear hear
liberation was now don't you know
it's a mainstream fashion
has been for decades
                    (they sd
                -but you see
she) interposed
            -liberating
            saturated fat from
            human ingestion
(because it produces
bad cholesterol
clogs arteries
expands skeletal waifs
into overweight blimps
            -could be perceived
            as a vegetarian plot!
(a well organized
conspiracy to remove
animal fat, flesh, other
disgusting buy products
for human consumption!

she) thought about visions
and versions of visions and
which version her intellect

measured compatible
with her daily life
she) posited priorities
           (those choices acted on
and reviewed her versions
of terrorists
and terrorist acts
connected to causes
espousing liberation and
sometimes thinly cloaked
as virulent inquisitions.

she) poems ii

munich - 5/23/87

long before she was able-
she) expected to move mountains with
her thoughts because they stood in her way.

she) discovered what avalanches
and too much rain could do to
a mountainside, and left them alone.

she) met another woman who
was earth-wise and sure-footed
plucking crystals from cliffs and lakes.

this earth woman told her about a
spider fall where marmots lived and
where a white chalk path from

another medicine life was hiding.
she) carried this knowledge back
with her across a great distance

and then settled herself into dreams
that drove her through different fields
over familiar mountains and deserts.

she) reached the western shore
of her homeland and
created herself once more.

#####

she) found images in
her mind of the
land of enchantment
her born to homeplace-
and how there was always
a mystery hovering
around the land
its huge spaces its

217

big skies and massive
clouds—

        all that power
on those mountain tops
leaning out to trap stars—
to root tribes to valley floors.

she) came upon the
lava beds of her early
childhood and teenaged
years where she had
picknicked and rounded up
cattle at branding time and
she) remembered how black
malpais whorls sustained
scattered grass clumps
grown out of abandoned seed

        wind blown seed
carried in maverick
dust funnels
deposited in cracks
crevices and lacey
openings of lava rock

        where crows and sparrows
        would never notice.

        ######

9/94

she) moved through days of
blackberry and vegetable patches
approaching another equinox

she) observed
net gains from spent days
abstracted memorable highlights
for further examination

218

some distant future-
rearranged / edited / added
before storing into
continuing memories.

sometimes
she) discarded many
days at once when
she) was unable to
alter their contents enough to
fit her ideal self image
or when
her day dreams
would not fit her
self prescribed formula of
is me: is not me:

######

12/8/93

she) resolved to express
her experience as it came
to her:
a series of aggregate thoughts

images piled one on another
abstract and concrete
modes of articulation
in the fullness of language
yet
paring description to
the most essential
the most important
the barest
molecule of a thought

she) assumed this was
a human method of
sorting and sifting the
elements of her living moments

she) supposed anatomy invaded
this symbolic denotation
only because
she) had been 'washed' into
this belief by
those who determine
these divisions among
life forms posited
at this stage/time/end of
the cosmos (at large
yet—human to be sorting
human to be naming—
to express her thoughtful
images some way.

######

10/31/95

she) stumbled across
pillow choked sobs and
found an old nightmare
buried beneath layers of
salt soaked tears
she) hummed a vacant
tune in a quiet voice-

**and this is the way
we wash our minds
and shine our souls. . .**

she) watched her
pumpkin and sweet
potato patches
cast long shadows
across orange harvest moons
and sandstone spires.

**and this is the way
we mend our hearts
and swallow our lives. . .**

she) nestled her body
next to his under
coverlets and quilts
recalling lean years
when nothing worked
quite the way
she) planned it.

backyard hammocks and
wilted marigolds belie
the yankee dollars that
put them there
on rusty days long past—

**and this is the way
the songbirds sing and
squirrels chatter. . .**

hiding disappointed
aftermaths cloudy skies and
moments best forgotten.
she) hugged herself
with rainbows
remembering orange lollipops—
the end for a new rhyme:

**and this is the way. . .
the way we play
today
today.**

she) navigated among the
objects in her local universe
determined to deepen her
experience in holograms

she) witnessed invisible
motions connecting events
but could only speak about

plums grapes and pineapples
being the same in the field
          (not after decaying into
individual atoms
but as they are now
blooming into tiny fruits
energy filled atom clusters
bursting toward ripe fulfillment
dreamed by tree vine and plant
all in a moment's work.

she) grasped hidden meanings
surrounding aboriginal dreamtimes;
in black elk's non-journey to the moon
how it was he found moonstones in
his pocket afterwards.

######

10/95-9/96

she) scooped up reams of words
splashed them into her brain
steeped her mind in
expanded concepts
long held captive within
isolated codes
then formed compound words to
contain precise denotations
for use in some future
waiting to be inhabited
with her gleanings and knowings.

she) remembered a
european legend that
told how the god of abraham
had cast a 'bringer of light'
out of the heavens
into the darkness below.
that legend holds
               (in thought

that in**deed** lucifer
was that god's creation.

she) pondered the reasons
for this mythical conflict.
this battle between
creator and created for
supremacy or primacy or
was it primal supremacy?

she) wondered if that primary
conflict was a resolution of
two clashing dynamic forces
polarized in such fashion
that the light bearer
                    (the lucifer
might have a unique purpose;
might reasonably be considered
a factor in the enlightenment
of humankind
for does not a lucifer-
a light bringer -illuminate
the surrounding darkness?

and did not lucifer's
brilliance blind those
who stared into his visage
too long and too deeply?
but those who turned
eyes and ears inward. . .
might discover a new image
a more ancient story
than ever suspected
by dreamers and visionaries
alike.

she) noted that
this diabolos—
            ('confuser' to the greeks-
set out to
disturb the peace to
break up 'happily ever after'
because no progress

no new thought can come
into being without disruption.

she) understood that
the seeds of change
were always considered
evil   -initially
but the angel of light
the renowned lucifer
is scapegoat **and**
potential redeemer.
we seek change and
transformation in all
          we do-
she) whispered to
the night and day. later

she) heard somewhere that:
          -contrast will feed us duality
          keep us bound between
          dark and light
          day and night
          but freedom dwells
          within the heart of love
          waiting—
          waiting to be embraced
          with delight
          outside this sight this
          all pervading light
          light bearer
          light bringer

she) could follow the form
of the argument but
her mind sent signals
to retreat into calmer realms—
places where castles
would not fall and
myth and legend remained
pure and untouched

she) cast doubts to the winds
cast fortunes in the sands

called time to rescue her
from indifference and subtleties
then bade lucifer remove duality
from all her enlightened moments.

######

8/95

she) decided that squeezing pearls
out of swine was more challenging
than remembering not to cast them
carelessly around
though on some days it felt
more like leading a horse
                          to water
                          to water
                          to water

                  on other days
she) found a particular mood
and just side stepped into it—
caught glimpses of actions
and reactions
she) wanted to change
could not determine how to
and left herself no pause
to find an easy way out.

she) examined all her things
those symbols of who
she) was
emanating from her mirrors

symbols for these times
these moments of her
earth journey and wondered
how she'd) managed to
create so much stuff!

######

9/16/96

she) called unhappy thoughts
into being and spent
them with careless abandon

she) wandered into her
mind fields and found
silver caskets holding
unformed ideas of
transition and transference.
only the most erudite and
blue blooded scholar can
shine through the dross
can rearrange a sentence
can commingle unlike terms
(split peas, granola, alabaster
marry haves with have-nots.

she) naively proposed
simple models-
the first class ingredients
of a good story line-
elevated miracles to promote
wonder and fascination
with sensible endeavors
mundane events and
tomorrow's minutiae.

she) hoped last week's
strawberry pie would retain
its vivid taste and color
for others besides herself
she) wished barbecued ribs
and baked beans held
nostalgia for more than
just a few others in
her local sphere.
most explanations were
generally risky

involved more than
spelling out images
and counting skeletons for
this week's hash-

she) had tasted heavenly hash
before but it wasn't what she'd
expected so she) gave up
the idea of sweet cherries
marshmallows and nuts
buried in jello
as a metaphor for
anything in her
daily life.

notes from central
missouri

1. mezcladas*
      (para gloria a.

we come to our histories
battered and bruised
with cuentas of a heritage
partially known to us.

gentes mezcladas we seek
our race, our rightful place
en el mundo y en la vida
where we find ourselves
passing — always passing
porqué — because
somos mestizos
exotic gene pools of
miscegenation.

high yellah's and golden browns
almond shaped green eyes
sin epicanthic fold
nosotros somos la raza nueva
and that's a fact
but we are still unaccepting
we are the walkin wounded
scarred by los 'others'
y our own gente — también
truly multicultural yet
ashamed of our bloodlines commingling
creates havoc inside us
produces fragmented identities
that claim and reject
this ethnicity or that race
until we become shattered
versions of our original selves.

2.
i'm black, filipina, mexican
and irish   (she sd
and my husband is black and japanese-
her brown skinned face framed
by rich black hair glowed with

pride and her dark eyes smiled
when she sd their babies
represented the world.

la raza nueva   (i sd
la raza de bronce grows
larger each day.
hijos del mundo mezclados
mixed race, mixed blood children
holding hands around the world.
la raza nueva
emerging slowly but
emerging none-the-less.

3.
we come to our histories
record them in print
and find they are
personal, political
and polemical.
para nosotros-
politics and polemics
hold hands these days
but are not las piensas
included in proper poetics-
(not allowed - do not fit
homeric or aristotelian
guidelines   -are
inappropriate subject matter
for the culture market
do not belong in harper's
atlantic monthly or
new yorker magazines.
politics and polemics
passing as poetry-
a senseless image
no hear, see, taste, touch
or smell to it at all

yet, passing carries
countless images
in its wake

denotes action
active movement
transition and
transformation:
thoughts into words
trains in the night
rivers into seas
earth through space
goddess as woman
women into goddesses
men into gods
god as man
persons into politics
politics as poetry.

a new form emerges as our histories
combine in this -the new world-
emerges along with la raza nueva
de los hijos del mundo
mezclados.
5/94

[*mezcladas: mixed blooded;
cuentas: stories;
gentes mezcladas: mixed blooded people;
en el mundo y en la vida: in the world and in life;
porqúe: because;
somos mestizos: we are mixed breeds;
sin: without;
nosotros somos la raza nueva: we are the new race;
los: the; y: and; gente-también: people-also;
la raza de bronce: the race of bronze;
hijos del mundo mezclados: mixed blooded children of the world;
para nosotros: for us;
las piensas: the thoughts;
la raza nueva de los hijos. . .: the new race of mixed blood children of the
world.]

2. ourstory
(for gerda lerner

centuries trickle across inked pages
crystallizing points of interest
selected by patriarchs of eras past
events culled to lionize or instruct
illuminate or inform

proprietary
and proper
pious ideals

the adventures and inventions
of super heroes of the day
engraved in stone
encoded on papyrus
inked on parchment
printed on paper
carved in clay

appropriately named histories
and so they are **his** stories

her stories, however, were excluded and yet
she) represents at least half of human kind
she) produces and feeds the human race -but
she) has been
omitted
denied
hidden
lost or
stolen
from his **story**-

rejoice!
her time has come-
her **story** begins to unfold

uncovered in events culled from eras past
brought to light by women of today
we reach for her adventures and inventions

her proprietary
      and proper
      pious ideals

as she lives them and gives them
to her daughters and granddaughters
for generations to come
      we are telling the
      many many stories
      of all she is doing
      of all she has done
and when we've gathered all the stories together
      of both matriarch and patriarch-
we will rename them **ourstory**.

7/93

3. to create a piece of art
      (for paul a.

pastiche: collage: construction
construct:
moment filled pages
minute filled papers
hours of moondays.
embraced by rainbows
four happy devas
come to mind
each master of
one single color
chide me to
remember to
be mindful of
their powers to:
sing color into being
spread color from
mountain top to
valley bottom
riding the four winds
singing their
naming songs
singing:
      remember me

> when you dance
> in my direction
> i am turquoise woman
> turquoise is my
> power stone
> turquoise mountain is
> my home

singing:
> i am yellow woman
> you will hear
> my siren song when
> you find my hidden gold
> when you face
> my yellow mountain
> remember my name

singing:
> coral mountain is
> my sacred place
> dancing sun rays
> into sundowns
> i am coral woman
> for your eyes
> to behold
> for your heart
> to remember

singing:
> you will remember
> my face and
> my ancient song
> when you look my way-
> i am white shell woman
> of the ageless dance
> and white shell mountain
> belongs to me

singing
always singing
their color songs:

> remember me

remember my song
my sacred color
my mountain home
remember my song
remember my color
remember my home
remember.

" . . .this poem merely turns
your head for
a moment, it
changes nothing. . .

(from "No Animals Allowed"
by gogisgi/carroll arnett-1994

4.
coyotes bark
in the evening
just after sunset

the neighbors
don't understand
coyotes at all

they set steel
traps instead
of planting

prayer sticks.

5.
cicada songs
rise and fall as
a giant sun ball
glows orange
sings red
bright and deep
becomes rose
then filters pinks
as it drops
into a turquoise
horizon.

south wind
bends corn tassles
skips sparrows across
tree tops
to chatter in
the front yard maples
and chase each other
in and out of
rain gutter nests.

barn swallows queue up
on the electric wire to
watch sunlight
shapeshift the day
into twilight
as this late
summer evening
slips across
central missouri.

messages (1988–1996)

journey's end
(santa barbara)

1.
any point on a circle
reflects any other point,

& i am reminded to notice
reflections i cast;
thoughts i would ignore
that were indeed
seeded, by me.

2.
neither fantasy nor reality
sit behind windows
of luck & circumstance

a bluejay feather falls
from a table top mountain
onto my bed quilt

four months to cover that distance
hundreds of events
between then
& now

3.
i watch shoppers browse
through 'indian country' -
my current home away
from rural life &
big city splendor in

this quiet town
bounded by mountain tops &
sea coast beaches
studded with stately palms
& eucalyptus groves.

this quiet town where
baked spanish tiles leap
from rooftop to rooftop

flowing redbrown under
muted greens of palm frond banners
that disguise new & old daily conflicts
tucked in every corner-
buried under old sidewalks
or in ancient gravesites of
those peoples who first
walked these hills &
fished the serene coastal waters.

4.
the freedom generation
haunts these latter
twentieth century days
with songs of then
reaching for songs of now;
use third world rhythms
out of mother africa
out of cajun bayous

and still
we don't know
"what it is. . ."
"where it is. . ."
"where we go from here. . ."

5.
full moon into
partial eclipse
like partial days
too busy to think
clear thoughts. . .

he sd) indigenous peoples
were reduced to week-end
spirituality & failed
bingo businesses
on the 'rez'

simon & garfunkel blend voices
'feelin groovy'
as i watch this
1982 central concert

tv replay of the 70's
& the 60's

those 60's days of
'bein all into peace &
love & hitchhikin coast to coast
- you know -
totally dropped out'   (she sd

6.
days fall into years
seasons change
march one into another

larry's piano sings
my 'sweet embraceable you'
from a hotel biltmore corner &
contentment hangs round
my shoulders
crowded with just enough
anxiety to place my reality
in perspective-

clearglass notes leaping
from piano strings
merge into melodies, into
harmonies-
& i try to unravel the miracle
of it all

cause / effect / effect / cause
repeat—replay

7.
'what is this thing
called love. . .'
a moment / day / year
embedded with life
brings brilliant suns
dark nights
& dreams
into being
even as stars laugh in galaxies

far far from here-
send light seeds

messages & memories
helter skelter through all space
spill super novas
through telescopes for
bright young astronomers
to measure, interpret, document-

cause / effect / cause
but they're still
"rioting in africa
& starving in spain
lala lala lala la. . ."

replay—repeat—repeat—replay
cause / effect

8.
the 80's end &
'where have all the flowers gone'?
have they bloomed all their blooms
or gone to seed?
& where do all the seeds
grow now?
(cause, effect
do they bloom in some
unknown place?
some fertile mind?

but the 80's
were all about
s p i r i t u a l i t y
yeah uh-huh
spirituality!!

9.
deep pacific blue
fades into the aquamarine
of my front yard pool.

surrounded by asphalt,
cement, stucco & glass
i look for grassy fields to
cast my reflections-
some fertile place nearby
that carries windsongs &
sunrays filled with magic seeds
for all of us.

11/88

wind song

my four wind brothers
tease me
chase me through
nearby cities and
laugh when they
frighten me.

they say i left them
out of my song last night
and i should
remember them
every time i offer
my smoke.

sometimes
they torment me
when i forget
to sing to them.
they push me around
dare me not to run and
hide from them.

other times they kick
sand in my face
or run cold fingers
under my clothes
across my skin
to scold me
to remind me of
their powers.

huk-ko* - now
i am sternly reminded
again!

today, i am wind
and rain
hugging cliff edges.
first, i kiss palm trees
oil pumps and
beach sand, then i

turn super highways
into mirrors
and sidestreets into
lakes.

today, i am wind
singing four winds songs
as my wind brothers
and i fly the 101
to ventura
together.

(2/89)

[*huk-ko - keres word meaning now]

unpacking the years
(for mother

in a mood
in a moment
blanketed in memories
a familiar odor returns
from a somewhere
tucked away in a photograph
album or the melody
of a song.

a gardenia night remembered:
late summer
dressed in black chiffon
her hair in a 1940's pageboy
held high with combs
frames her petite round face
and dark, dark eyes.

outside her reverie
a glen miller record
plays in the background,
creates a pleasant atmosphere
for her mid-morning
household chores,
carries her woman thoughts of
those somedays she dreamed about
and the romance times
she lived.

in a mood
in a moment
unpacking the years:
she remembers how it was
when she was young and vital
and her eyes sparkle dark
and lively

and the years
melt away until
she remembers

that day
is gone
and on this day
she tires too soon.

he calls to her
from another room
and she closes the
aging photo album
with a soft smile
leaving that mood
that moment
behind
for a little while.

3/90

song for the new age

the hopi say:
the two horn society
brought the last world to an end

but the two horns escaped
along with others
seeking a new way.

will the doom bringers
escape this time?
those modern two horn people with
all their magic making machines?

will it be possible to
create anew from the rubble
they leave behind?

new ways for old:
new ways for old:

there will always be
collectors of old ways
hoping to find a genie
hidden between the pages
behind an unused formula
or buried in some ancient
cure-all recipe for
body aches and
body pains.

new ways for old:
new ways for old:

come —smell an essence
dance a dervish;
come —breathe yourself
into heaven
exhale a —kiii aaaiii
chew the grey cactus
flesh until you
vomit your vision.

new ways for old:
new ways for old:

there is a recipe to transmute
lead into gold—   or into
golden dreams and fairy tales.
cross over the bed of hot coals
try the little death
make new gardens and
drive old cars
eat lots of müsli and
alfalfa sprouts.

no flesh, no flesh!
the gods abhor
eaters of flesh!

new ways for old:
new ways for old:

practice your yoga
three times a day
jog around the block
jog around the park
jog around the lake

remember to record
your dreams
examine your thoughts
confess your sins
flex your muscles twice
and feed your spirit thrice.

don't smoke tobacco
don't spit on the floor
don't speak to your neighbors
don't drink beer or whiskey
or wine or milk—
no sex   (if you must!
more than twice a month!

new ways for old:
old ways for new:

248

it makes no difference
which you choose.

new cells for old
this is what's true
new thoughts for old
this might work too.

new ways for old
old ways for new-
we can enjoy our
earth walk
whatever we do!

1993

> "the first derivative of velocity is
> acceleration; the second
> derivative of velocity is 'jerk'."
> (calculus theorem)

regarding chaos & order

soap bubbles call spectral
refractions into visibility.

cee equals two pie-are
limits line segments
approaching infinity.

to take the derivative of
a simple function is to
calculate certain shapes
or events
appearing in time and space.

hubbard sd) "randomness is death,
chaos is death. everything
is highly structured."
but barnsley's 'chance'
is only a tool, it leads to
the discovery of order
of structure arising out of chaos-
nature organizing itself
using simple physical laws
patiently waiting
for science to notice-
to have a look-see at living
phenomena so long ignored
yet still existing-
existing outside sterile
scientific laboratories.

2/90

leap frogging

into tomorrow on
yesterday's dream is
touted by those that know
as: unconscious activity.
never mind
forgetting your mind-
your moment to moment
fogged up hazy days.

daily diversions
come upon request but
disciplined selves become
successful beings
whatever our life's
choices—you say.

yet we stumble
through earth's mysteries-
naming, defining
claiming, refining
our days into years.

a distinction.
a division.
a judgement.
a chasm
between the unlearnéd
and the wise.

4/8/95

elemental happenstance
descended on a curve of
sunlight framing super heroes
and subterraneans alike.

batman, hercules and coyote
just want to be noted
for their earthy (earthly?
forays spread across
global topographies.

mythmakers only wish
to preserve great events
but are more concerned with
the creators of those events.

silly us scouring flea markets
attic dust or musty basements
in search of the sublime—those
connections between everything
in heaven/on earth.

maybe we forgot joseph knecht
and his intricate realities
confined to 'glass bead games'
filled with logical fugues
and empowered souls
moving through thin veils
between dimensions.

the ufo's of those times
(before mary made christ
and these times are
alien entities so large
earth eyes perceive only
blobs of light attached to
internal voices whispering-
singing.

silly us noting
orion's proximity to
the seven sisters

trying to locate all
those sky people
walking around down here.

the simple solutions
of super heros
rained frogs and locusts
for moses
dismembered and fossilized
giant ogres for warrior twins
with tricksters
appearing here and there
just to keep 'the show'
in extravagant production.

the stage was always
set for trickery. and how
well we tricked ourselves
into not remembering
who we truly are once
we have assumed our
local character roles.

all those energies
aimed at forgetting
everything we come from
just to dive into how it feels
'to be a rolling stone. . .'

can you imagine that?
a magical spirit
that allows speculation
beyond injunctions and
supreme courts of the mind?
and still pretends not to notice
what's really going on?

sir philip sidney reflects

serenade savages.
lull them.
teach them harmony
interspersed with
discordant tones.

plan raffles and
carnivals for the
rest of us to disturb
our equilibrium.

soothe our tired prattle
with goose berries and
rhubarb pies.

sweeten our sour
notes with
cane granules
whenever you can.

moonlit nights evade
city dwellers living
tv dramas into early
morning dreams.

daytime rushes beg for
more time for trips to
personal wisdom and
forgotten memories

extra minutes
stretch every hour to
include other dreams:
elegant constructs
for yoga movements
or rice paper drawings.

corners and sidewalks

today i gobbled morning sun
in exploration of other solar
revolutions   -those
chunks of being alloted to me.

i am surrounded by
dwellers in etheric space
(those places we created together
parallel universes coinciding
sashaying, twosteppin
mambo samba rhumba
bellydancin through
kaleidescopic melodies.

i cant get too serious over
violent beginnings and
violent endings like
two heads splitting or
berkeley divas
divebombing san jose
just to be noticed.
i remember how loud
we were-
naming ourselves
successors to the howlers
the isolationists
veterans all
of numerous
holocausts and
massacres.

we sing perdition
clothed in camouflage
eyes glazed
mouths laced shut
busy busy busy
times that fall
into the long
awaited new age-

ageless harbingers
sit on street corners
still playing off key
harmonicas
      (unharmed?
       or unharmonious??
wait for rusted tin cups
to capture hard cash
clinking coins clattering
out of anywhere onto
cold con-creeeete
         those
cee-ment sidewalks still
shuffling winos and billionaires
      together
under skyscraper monuments.

7/95

saturday's children

"monday's child is fair of face
tuesday's child is full of grace
wednesday's child is full of woe
thursday's child has far to go
friday's child is loving and giving
saturday's child must work for a living
a child that's born on the sabbath day
is fair and wise and good and gay."

(anonymous nursery rhyme

crystaled vagueries of
tortured moments and minds
settle on mint juleps with
lemon twists—then
sing multitonal songs.

though
we search souls for
everlasting understanding
along with the familiar sight of
an elm tree
a lotus blossom or
that solitary pine
courageously guarding
a spare rocky mountaintop

instead—
more often than not—
we find distorted interpretations
among bramble thickets
rose thorns
and blackberry patches
scraping flesh and bone.

saturday's winners
are not easily located
so few are there to seek out.
saturday's children must
labor endless cycles

are permitted few
unencumbered frolics or
good luck lucky star days
to revel in at will.

saturn's day demands
grind wheel noses of
all his subjects
                    insists on
absolute attention to minutiae
and glum repetition of all tasks

jungle backpacking trips
spring woods mushroom hunts
or making out at the new
drive-in movie theater after 10 -
15 - 20 years of together nesting
are just nominal events
in human lives.

            'semper fi gyrene'
your personal peek into
the bowels of hell was
                    just a blip
on the big screen
        of personality—

remember "sticks and stones"?
and our monumental memoriums to
        unjust slaughter ?
well—name calling and all that
crumbles against weeping walls
—those ebony granite slabs
holding the dead
            transformed

        become:
tuesday's grace filled children

        re membered.

2/26/95

on reading of your death in poetry flash
(for ricardo sánchez

buckle up your life-
your abused heart
and soul
head for the hills vato*
la migra always wants
your body, pero
your poetic mind
siempre siempre
belongs to nuestra gente
aayyyy- hermano triste
hermano alegre
me falta lengua
  palabras
  aire
  dichos
  y tiempo
para reconstruír
  sus "dales"
  sus vidas evoking
  multicultural clashes-

te encuentras
en la calle
algunas años pasados en
un día llena del sol
y te me pregúntas
como estoy
y empezamos una
conversación acerca
nos hijos our daily lives
and loving hates
our cancerous angers
chicano peacemaking wars
con life busting
adventures into
dangerous unknown days
comin at you
  a su família
  at all of us

        que te quieras
        y no te quieras
        también
hijo del paso del norte
chicano poet from
the land of in between
te cantas bién
y ahora
vaya con los espíritos
del mundo
            del cielo
            del calle
y bién viaje vato
adónde vas.

9/10-95

[*vato: comrade; la migra: immigration;
pero: but; siempre: always;
nuestra gente: our people;
hermano triste: sad brother; hermano alegre: glad brother;
me falta lengua: i have no language; palabras: words; aire: air;
dichos: sayings; y tiempo: and time; para reconstruír: to reconstruct;
sus "dales": your gifts; sus vidas: your lives;
te encuentras: i met you; en la calle: in the street;
algunas años pasados en: some years ago on;
un dia llena del sol: a sun filled day;
y te me pregúntas: and you asked me; como estroy: how i was;
y empezamos una: and we began a;
conversación acerca: conversation about;
nos hijos: our children; con: with;
a su familia: at your family; que te quieras: who love you;
y no te quieras: and who don't love you; también: also;
hijo del paso del norte: son of the northern pass;
te cantas bién: you sing well; y ahora: and now;
vaya con los espíritos: go with the spirits; del mundo: of the world;
del cielo: the sky; del calle: the street;
y bién viaje vato: and good journey comrade;
adónde vas: wherever you are.]

on poetics

we come
to discuss our genius—
our lucid moments
bound by our heritage

we push our words
into silken baskets of
acid free rag bond
and proudly send them
off to market

these idioms of our
inventive minds—
      our words incarnate
      our words made flesh
      our symbol forms
emerging into substance
all the while assuming
future generations
      (our children's children's children
will find us clever and erudite
as forgers of new metals
extracting rare essentials
from ordinary ores
to birth new themes
      forms, rhythms
that enchant or startle
      expecting
      these mental treasures
      to be as carefully preserved
      as any stone stelae's glyphs
      have been.

9/95

recitations

bob kaufman
roamed the streets
of north beach
reciting poetry to others
for drinks and smokes
to the sky
the ocean and
himself for food

he was a poetic genius
they sd)

i met him one night when
he came into the coffee gallery
walked up to me
sd) can i read some poems man?
i sd) go ahead man
on stage behind the mike
shoulders squared carefully
glaze-eyed and dignified
he recited eliot's prufrock
in entirety. from memory.
sd) thank you man and walked
out into the san francisco night.

some years later
his missus began appearing
at poetry readings wanting
to recite some of bob's poems

to save his poetic genius
we sd)

2/95

snapshots
(for al young

i remembered
loving mexico so much
i wanted to live there
forever but i couldn't
talk any of my husbands
(first, third, fourth or
last into it. i wanted
to move there until the trip
in 1985 when i discovered
how awful it was for indios
down there-
especially mexico d.f.*
it was the day we took
a side trip from d.f. to taxco
and the 'i'm proud to be mestizo'
tour guide lectured us about
touristas giving 'spare change'
to those dark skinned mothers
with por favor eyes staring
up at us from their begging
crouches on the sidewalks.
-you only encourage them
to come in from the pueblas
and sully our streets with
poverty and sadness (he sd
just ignore them—please—
i want to keep my bonita city
clean!

[*mexico d.f.: mexico city;
mestizo: mixed breed;
touristas: tourists;
por favor: please;
pueblas: villages;
bonita: beautiful]

celebrating women's stories
(for diane s.

this night's moon
sings in the quarter heaven
calls fancy to name our mothers.

sun calls cloud covers out
of southern caves pretending
to need shadows   -intending to
gamble with rain god instead.

spider hangs undisturbed in
the central quadrant
busy with creation
busy with generating material goods
spinning nets tapestries blankets
baskets sandals shirts skirts
mats and shades.

rainbows dance rainbows
scatter colors onto human aspirations
spread laughter and harmony
on all who trespass
against themselves—expecting despair.

rain drops moisten dry lands
enable farmers to hope
give birth to tadpoles
chase birds into hiding and
fill creeks with gurgles and splashes.

we gather together in comraderie
embrace friendship and joy filled memories
celebrate womanhood—human experience
and our lives as light filled beings
awakened.

4/27/96

memo to myself

i pace my space.
my place.
my energies linger on
filaments attached
to familiar things.
a full length mirror
on a door
a bathroom shelf
a pair of curtains
some old tablecloths
bits of selves i
wore with hesitation
or willful certitude

i climb mountains and
more mountains
wanting to reach
god heights / find
lovers' leaps instead

fragments of other moods
unwind out of memory
recall other days
waiting to happen
in other combinations
daynights
nightdays
locating future selves
in celestial patterns
hanging wistfully now
in some dear past
a once was time
i felt harmony
on my fingertips.

11/95

from spirit to matter

beyond january sunsets
through golden doors of mercy
beside empty gardens lie
mysterious mountains of wonder

around timeless treasures hidden
throughout the ancient realms
among carpenters, cobblers and assassins
life blooms brilliant and wicked all at once

underneath pale green rainbows
below lemon trees and haystacks
behind summer's picket fences
masks and shields hold heaven hostage

before hallowed altars
over blood caked ruins
of forgotten eras; of peopled nations;
lovers struggle to nourish an unknown future.

between the years we've lived and loved
before we named and claimed each other
within our fantasies of selves
god stuff swirled as invisible thought waiting to be born.

11/95

carol lee sanchez was born and raised in rural new mexico and is mostly of laguna pueblo and lebanese heritage. from 1976 to 1985 she was a member of the san francisco state university faculty in san francisco, california. while there, she taught courses in american indian studies, ethnic studies and womens studies and chaired the american indian studies program in 1979 and 1980. from july of 1976 through july of 1978, sanchez held the position of statewide director of the california poets in the schools program. her poetry has been widely anthologized and her volumes of published poetry include: *conversations from the nightmare*, 1975 (casa editorial), *message bringer woman*, 1977 (taurean horn press), and *excerpts from a mountain climber's handbook*, 1985 (taurean horn/out west ltd). *she) poems*, a chicory blue press chapbook, was published in 1995. sanchez moved from santa barbara, california in 1989 to a farm in central missouri where she grows vegetables, reads, writes, paints and teaches short courses at the community college in sedalia and conducts poetry workshops in nearby grade schools.

cover design and artwork by gary whitney
photo by thomas e. allen
typeface: palatino
2000 copies printed by Thomson-Shore

correspondence should be addressed to:

Taurean Horn Press
1355 California St. #2
San Francisco, CA 94109

Taurean Horn Press
1355 California St. #2
San Francisco, CA 94109

Name_____

Address_____

_____

Please send me _____ copy/copies of *from spirit to matter*
by carol lee sanchez. I have enclosed a check/money order
for _____. (Make checks to Taurean Horn Press.)

The Arithmetic:

_____ copies of *from spirit to matter* @ $14.95 _____

+ $3.00 handling & postage   _____
(for 5 copies or under—for more than 5
        please write THP first)
+ tax (8.5% for SF Bay Area residents—   _____
        8% for other California residents)

TOTAL   _____

Please allow 2-3 weeks for shipping.